Ed McNamara has been both a dental patient of mine and a sportswriter for "Newsday" for 30 years. Via email, I sent him this early story and asked for suggestions. He gave his permission to use his reply, which also acts as a prelude.

Ron:

I think maybe you went into the wrong profession. Comedy writing suits you very well, and maybe you could have been another Larry David. I can't curb my enthusiasm. I thought it was a terrific story — tales of suffering, and bizarre pain at that — are the funniest, which says a lot about our species. I made hardly any changes (no sentences were harmed or amputated in the editing of this story), just little style things and removing a few extraneous words. It's certainly good enough to publish as is, and laugh-out-loud funny. The fact that it's true makes it even better, though I cringed at your situation. What an absolute nightmare. And it will prevent me from taking a stress test unless I am put in a straitjacket and drugged. I thought that all it involved was running on a treadmill or something like that.

Send me more of them. It was fun to read. — Ed

RON'S RAMBLINGS

Ron Salmonson

Deb,

It has been an absolute pleasure treating you for the past thirty-five years

Ron Salmonson

Lulu Publishing Services rev. date: 8/15/2013

ACKNOWLEDGMENTS

This book would not have been written without the loving support and endorsement of my wife Iris, who encouraged me to put on paper, the stories that unfold on these pages. Iris also deserves recognition for her computer skills, being my sounding board, and the tireless, tedious hours editing these ramblings. In addition, special thanks for her cover and all the art work.

I also would like to thank my neighbor, retired English teacher Marsha Osrow, who jump started my writings. She gave me the inspiration and motivation to compose the first of these off-the-wall articles for our Hamlet community journal. Marsha skillfully guided and coddled me through my first articles.

I again thank my wife for pushing me to join the writing club at Valencia Falls in Delray Beach, Fla. where we winter. These weekly meetings took me from my kindergarten level writing skills to where I am presently. I thank each member of this group, but especially recognize Howard Gleichenhaus and Joyce Saltman who are the big "kahunas" in the club. Some of the unusual themes came about because of class assignments i.e. write about flowers, a neighbor, a thank you note, alternately interspersed with free-lance writings.

Particular thanks to my kindergarten and third grade friends Gary Harrison and Michael Kramer for their inputs, in chronicling our life stories. Mary Stoll, who as editor of the N.Y. State Dental Journal published many of my dental articles; Phyllis August, who provided material for one of my essays and the many friends and patients, too numerous to mention, who expressed their delights in reading these pieces and suggested I publish these stories.

"If I write something that I think is good, then somebody will like it. Maybe not everybody, but that won't matter."
– Ron Salmonson

(sillysal@optonline.net)

CONTENTS

A JEWEL OF A STORY

Preventative medicine is the established philosophy in today's health care climate. With a familial history of cardiovascular issues, I thought it would be prudent to take a baseline stress test, while I felt totally healthy, in case future problems arise. At the age of 62, I took a nuclear stress test at my local cardiologist's office. The monitoring technician stopped the procedure because my blood pressure was too high. The physician thought it was best, to follow up with an angiogram, to determine the cause of this elevation. He said, "I suspect you have a blocked coronary artery."

I had to find an interventional cardiologist to perform the angiogram. I learned there are web sites that keep statistics of treatments, both by the cardiologist and hospital. It was like looking up batting averages, to determine the facility and doctor you'd choose. The stats were listed with the patient having no symptoms and when the patient was in distress. Since my procedure would be quasi-elective, I had ample time to select. By chance I chose a cardiologist, who happened to be my son's friend, with great statistics. His hospital was located an hour from home, near Roosevelt Field, which also has a great shopping mall. I was never

1

too sure if this mall influenced my wife's decision to go with this hospital.

It certainly was weird being semi-conscious, while the cardiologist ran a wire through my groin that roamed my heart, as I watched the monitor. The angiogram revealed I needed one stent, which the cardiologist placed seamlessly. When the doctor finished, he stepped outside the operating room to inform my wife, "Everything went well. They'll remove the catheter and you can see him."

The physician's assistant, who removed the catheter from my groin, nicked my femoral artery — *all hell broke loose.* I was still partially sedated but felt a tremendous amount of pressure on my crotch. When I looked up, there were loads of medical personnel hovering between my legs.

My wife, who expected to shop after meeting with the doctor, saw from afar, something wasn't kosher. They of course wouldn't allow her to see me. Later she told me, "I was so upset, I called our son and asked him to get to the hospital ASAP."

Eventually, they clamped the artery and the bleeding stopped, but a large amount of blood had pooled inside my crotch. The medical staff had a pow-wow to determine the best course of action. The cardiologist, surgeon, urologist and internist agreed the best treatment would be to let the blood resorb naturally, without further intervention.

I was then transferred to cardiac intensive-care to be monitored. This was due to the extensive internal bleeding and recent stent placement. The doctor said, "This area of the hospital is where patients are watched most carefully." After a few hours, the sedative wore off and I woke in the middle of the night and looked around. I was the only patient not looking close to death. It was an absolutely, surreal, out-of-body experience.

Wakening from this dreamlike stupor, I took a look at what was going on down there. They had placed a catheter in my male member that contributed to my discomfort. Everything was very bizarre. I was totally black and blue from my waist to my thighs. In the middle of this area, I swore I saw what looked like a black rat lying there. This was quite upsetting because I didn't remember giving permission to do a penis transplant with an Afro-American.

By myself in the middle of the night, with a bunch of pre-dead people, I realized I had to talk to somebody. I pressed the emergency button. In comes this attractive female nurse in her late twenties who asked, "What's the problem?" Now this young lady greatly trained in cardiology and probably not used to a cardiac patient, who quizzed, "Is it normal to have a black rodent lying between my legs?" Astonished, she looked at the area and of course said, "In my experience everything looks normal!" I go nuts (pun intended) and asked, "This is **NORMAL**? I want to see an urologist ASAP!"

I thought since its black and showing no signs of life, maybe my unapproved transplant might be dying. The next day at 8 a.m. Dr. Edelstein head of urology, examined me and assured, "All is within normal limits, for the bleeding I had."

Now my jewels (penis, scrotum, testicles; I often wonder how the area got its name) swelled to the size of cantaloupes. It was very, very difficult to walk, or go to the bathroom. I had to hold my jewels in both hands, to move with minimal pain. I asked the urologist, "What do you recommend to support these new appendages? Was there a special jock strap to handle the task?" He said, "The best thing to wear is tight undergarments. Women's underwear would definitely do the trick." Since I was always somewhat intrigued how this soft, silky material would feel, I gave it a try.

My wife's underwear, average in size, couldn't come close to supporting my new accompaniments. I had many, many lady friends offer me their undies. I even tried a few thongs to see if they'd work. From the back, my pants looked absolutely gorgeous on me. The thongs however, were just too uncomfortable. The panties that fit best were from my 400-pound cousin. Even with these large "bloomers" I had to use both hands to assist my new additions. My arms ached and my walk resembled a cross between an ape's and an elephant's.

After being prodded every fifteen minutes in the cardiac intensive-care unit, it was a major relief to go home. My wife and I discussed if we should contact a malpractice lawyer. After much deliberation, she decided it was in our best interest to document the state of affairs. She got our camera and photographed me in various positions. Our son, who just happened to stop by, saw these pictures. This now confirmed his thoughts, that his parents were perverts.

At this time my jewels fit the perfect description of "Elephantiasis." These pictures will be published in the September 2010 issue of National Geographic. By the way, I do have a few copies of this issue, in case anyone wants a look. Incidentally, I did decide this wasn't malpractice.

It took about three months for the cantaloupes to resolve, going through the smaller sizes of grapefruits, oranges, peaches and use your imagination. The color of the traumatized region changed from Afro-American to Chinese to Caucasian.

When they got down to the size of oranges, I went back to work. I'm a dentist and work sitting down, treating patients almost completely reclined. Some of my patients have been with me over thirty years. I told several of them what transpired and asked if they would mind moving a little away from me, so I could put my jewels on their chair. In this way, the patient also could feel more in control of their dental work, in case I hurt them.

Eventually, everything healed normally. I still subscribe to the philosophy of preventative medicine, and thank goodness for that, because if I didn't, I'd never have this "jewel" of a story.

OLDER THAN MY DAD

Today **is the** day I am older than my Dad. Yesterday would have been the last day of my life, if I were him. How did this happen that I became older than my father? Now, every picture taken of me, I am older than him!

I took my Dad's photograph off the wall and stared at it. The picture captured his annual carving of the Thanksgiving

turkey. He's looking directly at me, since I took the photo. It's been a long time since he died, thirty-five years, but I still remember the milestones. When I think of him, I can't see his face anymore. I see this picture of him in a frame.

"My father is bigger than your father." I often said, because he was! He was a child of the depression, uneducated and did manual labor his entire life. When asked what he did, he'd smile and say, "I'm a M.D. - a mattress dealer." He literally took apart old mattresses - cotton, coverings, and made them into bales. The cotton bales weighed around eight hundred pounds, which he muscled at work. These textiles were sent to second hand manufacturers who converted these materials into beds or pillows. He worked with my uncle for over forty years. Their plant was in the heart of the dangerous Bed–Stuy section of Brooklyn. On rare occasions even though my uncle always carried a gun, they were robbed and beaten.

A large man over six feet tall, two hundred pounds, my father Rube was solid as a rock. He worked twelve hour days, in bitter cold and jungle heat. Then, there were no such things as heating or air conditioning. His hands were mammoth and thickly callused. He never, ever wore gloves because they didn't make them big enough. Even as an adult, two of my fingers equaled one of his.

He always ate alone, caringly served by my mother, because he came home too late to eat with the family. My father Rubin, was never around. St. Rube (the name earned for living with my mother) always worked. He was invisible during the daytime. Daytime was ruled by my mother and Dad came out at night. Darkness brought out my father with his regal and unspeakable powers. I always sensed his enormous love and cherished the safety of his arms. Though he seldom spoke, I always felt his affection by his actions and his encouraging words.

By his simple eloquent example, this unschooled man taught me to respect all forms of work. Because of him, I have total admiration for the common worker, at every level. This gentle man left a rich inheritance by his actions. He didn't tell me how to live; he showed by example.

One summer when I was fifteen, my Uncle Phil was badly beaten. I (Ronny) didn't know about the attack and had to work with my cousin Nonny, his son to help out. We were only told Phil needed hernia surgery. This eye opening experience became a driving force, in showing me the importance of education. I was scared stiff I'd have to do this type of work for life. Getting an education was the only thing, my father demanded. It was not negotiable!

My father's earliest memory was at three, the day his mother died. I always thought it was a reach that he could go back that far, but my father never lied. She died falling out the window of their third floor apartment. She'd been cleaning windows and there were no guard rails. Ruby hid under the bed during the commotion. My Dad never let my mother or his kids clean the windows in our six floor apartment. Dad always did them.

Rube was a child of the Depression and had to quit school in the eighth grade. He worked his entire childhood. Because of this, he didn't want me to work during mine. I did anyway (at fourteen) and deep down I think he was pleased, although he never said.

Dad loved helping others and being a Mr. Fix-it. He always asked friends and relatives if there was anything needing repair. Ruby was painstakingly meticulous, and never charged. His work was flawless and fixing things in solitude (my father was hard of hearing and that contributed to his being quiet) fit his temperament perfectly. He taught me your work projects become your signature; therefore always sign them well. Regrettably, I could never fix anything well enough for him, so after a while I gave up. He planned to open a Mr. Fix-it shop in retirement, but he never lived long enough. The day he retired, he got sick, and then fought a one year losing battle to lymphoma.

Dad died with dignity. At the end, Rube was hospitalized

at the NIH in Washington, D.C. and received experimental chemotherapy. We made our weekly six hour treks from New York to D.C. and stayed the weekends. Dad wasn't religious and didn't turn to it at the end. He never asked "Why me?" It wasn't until I witnessed my Dad's passing, did I know what it means to die with grace. He was valiant in the face of death. Even at the end of his life, he never stopped being a father and educating his children. He didn't want us to disrupt our lives, by visiting him. He pleaded, "We must get on with living our lives."

I carefully take his photograph and place it back on the wall. The living change physically, but photos do not. The images of our departed loved ones are fixed in our minds, from our treasured photos. They never ever change. Is this part of nature's grand design?

My father would have been pleased that I have surpassed his age. Every parent hopes their children live longer than they. It's natural when you pass that moment, to reflect upon it. I am very proud that some of his legacies are replicated in me and my offspring.

AN 1822

Early in my dental career, whenever I had a bad day, I'd call my local friend and fellow dentist, Dr. Joe Salvado. Joe's office was five blocks away and we both had home offices. He would invariably cheer me up and render my problems inconsequential, compared to his. I was the rookie in the neighborhood, he the seasoned dentist. He opened his office three years before mine, and always gave the appearance of being a smooth, sophisticated practitioner.

In theory Joe and I should have been competitors in dentistry, but I never felt that way whatsoever. When I opened in 1973, Joe took me under his wing and showed me around. Soon after we arrived, he invited my wife and I to our first party in our new community. Shortly afterwards, we reciprocated and had our single friend for dinner. He became a Godparent to our two young sons. They played ball, horsed around and laughed non-stop. He was a skilled and caring dentist, and we had lots in common, i.e. sports and partying. In particular, we all loved to laugh. Dr. Joe marched to his own drum and created some very funny music.

Joe often could be absolutely outrageous. To this day whenever I think of him – I can't help smiling.

Joe had a punching bag in the basement of his home office. If he had an exceptionally stressful time working on a patient, he'd say, "The suction isn't working properly. I'm going downstairs to fix it." He'd go down, take off his dental tunic and beat the crap out of his punching bag. After getting out his frustrations, he'd towel off, return to the office, unbeknownst to the patient what transpired.

Dr. Salvado had some tough times handling the many problems of the profession. The biggest problem is trying to be perfect, when often you're working on a moving target. Dentistry has been likened to watch repair, but doing it under water. You're working in small confines, limited openings, gagging, large tongues, and microbes. Often you're trying to calm the fears of people who don't want to be there, while struggling to stay on time.

Dr. Salvado also had some health issues and left dentistry a number of times. While away, he tried acting, sales, nutrition (got his Masters), personal training and taught yoga. In between these various endeavors, he returned to dentistry two or three times.

Joe had heart problems from childhood, due to a bout with rheumatic fever, which damaged one of his valves. Recently, he had successful open heart surgery to replace this defective valve. Three months after surgery, Joe stopped by my busy office, after visiting his widowed father. Dr. Salvado marched into my dental operatory and gave a warm hello. Joe, always the bachelor, told us he's doing great. Then in front of my patient and dental assistant, he described his first date, after open heart surgery. It was with a brand new lady that he had never gone out with. He expressed in graphic detail, his thought process and worries regarding his newly repaired heart and having sex, after surgery. - Absolutely hilarious!

Dr. Joe was out of dentistry for seven years, when I received a phone call asking for a favor. Joe lamented "My eighty-eight year old father's gigantic bridge, I did twenty years ago is failing." His father lived near my office and Joe wanted to use my place, to redo this complex dental prosthesis. His father had a host of medical problems, including cardiac issues. I replied, "Gladly, I'll make sure I'm at the office when you're working on him." Joe had an ambivalent relationship with his Dad, who was upset with him for a variety of reasons, including leaving dentistry.

Dr. Joe had a ton of disadvantages doing dentistry at this point in time. He'd been out of the profession many years and technology had changed drastically. Besides being out of practice, my equipment was set up for a righty and he was lefty. Everything was awkwardly on the wrong side! Joe also didn't know where anything was. In addition, he had to do a difficult molar root canal because his father couldn't afford a specialist.

I gave Joe my finest dental assistant Margaret, who had been doing dentistry for thirty years. She was completely familiar with the room and together we hoped, they could complete this complex work. Their sessions went on for weeks. One day, as the office and waiting room were chockfull, a crisis unfolded. During root canal treatment, I heard a panicked Joe call out, "Dad, Dad are you all right?" Joe thought his father was having a heart attack and lost control. Immediately, we called 911 for an ambulance. Instantly, I ran into their room and saw Dr. Joe, now holding his chest. Dr. Joe was also having trouble breathing. Terror was rampant as I yelled, "Call 911 again for a second ambulance." Fortunately, the two ambulances arrived in no time. The turmoil didn't bode well with the patients in the waiting room, as they heard and witnessed the emergencies. Both Salvados were raced to Mather Hospital. Unbelievably, it turned out to be a double anxiety attack, one triggering the other. Luckily both patients didn't need any real medical intervention!

The Salvado men are special in my dental career because they pulled "An 1822" (911 X 2.) Never in my practice have I even once called 911. I still wonder if I were a patient where these potentially life threatening events occurred, if I'd ever return.

Weeks later father and son, all smiles, returned and resumed their dental treatment. Fortunately, the bridge was almost done. I now was considerably more nervous and listened intensely as they worked. Joe had difficulty inserting the bridge because his father's tongue got in the way. Anatomically, when a person loses a lot of teeth, the tongue which is muscle, helps out in chewing. As a result his father's tongue became humongous. Frustrated, Dr. Salvado said to his elderly father in front of my assistant "Dad, Dad would you get that big huge tongue out of the way! No wonder why Mom stayed with you all those years!" My fifty year old assistant almost fell off her chair. The entire office also heard what transpired. I can still hear the roars and roars of laughter echoing off the walls!

To date, the Salvados' hearts are ticking and still take care of one another. - Fighting with each other every day.

50TH ANNIVERSARY OF BEING IN JAIL

I **still remember** the awful feel and sound of the cold handcuffs ratcheting around my wrists. I had expected them to hurt more than they did. The cuffs were made for an adult. I was only sixteen and so thin at 6'1" and 140lbs. It was Nov. 28th 1961, the day after Thanksgiving. It was the absolute antithesis of Thanksgiving, the worst and longest day of my life!

The New York Post, Daily News and New York Times headlined, "Five senior Brooklyn high school star athletes caught stealing, exiting Midwood H.S." Serendipitously, the police had been cruising the area, when the five of us came out the school's back door. I can still hear the sirens screeching, as two officers pulled their guns, and told us, "Drop your stuff and put your hands up!" It seemed like in no time, a second squealing police car arrived with its sirens also blasting. The strobe lights were blinding and the sirens deafening. It was surreal. I thought this must be a dream or a movie. I got lightheaded and had trouble breathing.

Three of us, were starters on our high school basketball team. The fourth was captain of the swimming team and the fifth stole a gigantic set of keys from the school's janitor. These "capers" as we called them, started months earlier. A few of our other friends were also involved. We rotated randomly, depending on who was available, and who was up for the thrill. We'd sneak into the pitch dark building, and stealthily roam the school. We got "high", from the excitement of the escapades. I still remember the unbelievable quietness. The only sound I heard was the thunderous pounding of my heart, exploding in my chest.

Absurdly, we went to the gym and played basketball. (with no lights) Our capers then graduated. Since no one was around, we started to steal things. We took sneakers, jocks, practice jerseys etc. We thought about taking tests, changing grades, but never did. The day we got caught, this intelligent, seasoned criminal, proudly wore his Midwood basketball jacket, with his name embroidered on the front. I'm sure the coat drew some laughs, from the police officers at the 63rd precinct.

The police called for a paddy wagon, since there were five of us. It arrived with other criminals already in the patrol wagon. They handcuffed me to a huge, frightening, thirty year old motorcyclist. My 6'7" 225lb. crazy teammate Mark was paired with a very small, thin drunk. Since the wagon was a full, there were no consecutive seats in the vehicle. Mark and his new acquaintance sat across the aisle from one other. Their handcuffed arms hung over the aisle. As the paddy wagon turned, insane Mark pulled this criminal out of his seat, landing him in the aisle.

The sequence of events from finger printing, photos, and booking is meant to degrade the criminal. I remember trying to wash the black ink off my fingers. I couldn't get it off. It was like a tattoo, but the real tattoo was officially embedded in my brain forever. The chapter of my youth was now permanently closed from these devastating events. It was shut by the deafening sound of the jail door being slammed!

Around 1:00AM, our parents arrived at the station house. I dreaded this as much as my arrest. My mother cried pitifully with my father steadfastly at her side. My mother was flabbergasted and carried on, louder than all the other parents combined. From experience, I knew what she'd say next. She then delivered her line, as if it were a Broadway show. Her recurrent mantra, "What did I do to deserve this?" I just lowered my eyes to the ground.

Overnight, we were held in the precinct jail. My wacky eighteen year old (NY State legal drinking age at the time) accomplice Mark told the police, "He didn't like jail. They had the wrong kind of bars there." The five of us were separated and interrogated for hours. The cops inquired "How many times did we break in? What else did we steal? Did we steal any tests? Were others involved?" Independently, we told the truth, except no one squealed on our other partners in crime.

All five were thrown out of Midwood, sent to five different high schools and couldn't compete in sports at these new schools. Most of our scholarships were canceled. The infamous five were embarrassed, forever pointed at, and treated as social pariahs. We were assigned probation officers, whom we met weekly. At these meetings, I met a whole new group of people. Unfortunately, they were from the pits of society. I was completely crushed.

If you want to know who your friends are, get a jail sentence. Nobody knows you when you're down and out. While I went to jail, my whole family also went to jail. They had to deal with the humiliations, explanations, and costs. I became obsessed to prove this deviant episode was a one-time slip up. It became a driving motivation for future achievements.

There are some side bars worth mentioning. Mr. Fried, our hard-nosed basketball coach was extremely supportive and broke down in tears, when we spoke. He tried his utmost to save my scholarships. He also attempted to make me feel better saying "He would want someone like me to marry his daughter." I cried too. The depleted team still came in fifth in the NYC championships. I never again played organized basketball.

I was accepted (without a hitch) to the State University at Buffalo and rebounded to have a wonderful, well rounded four years. I joined a fraternity, had unbelievable roommates and met my future wife. Do I believe in fate, kismet? Not sure, but I would've never gone to Buffalo, and probably never have met my wife. (best thing that ever happened to me) My life would have never turned out the way it did, if I hadn't gotten caught and spent time in jail.

"Are there some defeats that are greater triumphs than victories?"

A DENTAL FETISH

The post extraction visit was within normal limits, except for one feature. Mrs. Becker was totally black and blue. She looked like I hit her a few times with a baseball bat. Her face resembled a *piñata*. Of course, she wasn't a great advertisement for this dentist, in her retirement community. Therefore I pleaded, "If anyone asks, who's your dentist – tell them it's Dr. Zahn." (He's my competitor down the road.)

Let's now go back about ten years, to the start of this story. Mr. and Mrs. Bob Becker were recommended, through word of mouth, by a retired dentist who lived in their over fifty-five year old community. At seventy, Bob recently retired from managing (forty years) a very successful dental laboratory in Queens, N.Y. He missed the work and action greatly. Bob was a soft spoken man who talked very, very slowly. In my mind, I'd be finishing his sentences before he did, as we all do at times. Since I had a busy practice, I had trouble listening to him.

His wife Edna was seventy-four, frail and frightfully thin. She had no eyebrows and wore an extremely ridiculous blonde wig that was appropriate for a thirty year old. Edna looked like a cartoon character, possibly Dagwood Bumstead's wife Blondie. She was joined to Bob at the hip, married fifty years and appeared very subservient. Another distinctive feature was her red brown blotchy skin. She was on long term blood thinners contributing to her numerous sizable bruises. It was the worst case, I had ever seen. She could easily have been a "poster girl" for the major blood thinners, Plavix or Coumadin. I later found out, they had no children and not many relatives.

Mr. Becker was extremely prideful of his career in dentistry. He would constantly bring his dental lab tools and memorabilia from his lifetime of work. His collection could qualify for the Dental Hall of Fame. Most of these items however, were so obsolete even George Washington's dentist wouldn't look at his stuff. But what a passion he had! Every time he'd talk about something he fabricated or invented, his eyes would get misty and he'd go into a dreamlike state, typical of dental bliss.

Mr. Becker of course, fabricated all of Edna's numerous crowns and was very proud of her complete set of thirty-two teeth. She'd never lost one, not even a wisdom tooth. Let me concur, she did show all her teeth, but it reminded me of "Chiclets."

The three of us got along delightfully, especially when they met my son who was in dental school. Bob felt completely comfortable he had found an office, which also shared his passion for dentistry. He was in "dental nirvana" and adopted us into their "dental family." Everyone knows someone, who dreads the dentist so much they cry when they have to go. The Beckers had the opposite problem. They enjoyed going to the dentist so much, they cried when they had to leave!

Unfortunately, Edna developed an acute case of "acid reflux." In severe cases, patients will repeatedly regurgitate a very strong acid (hydrochloric.) Over time this acid causes tremendous tooth break down, to the point of dissolving the entire tooth. The

Beckers recognized this problem and consented to do whatever is necessary (i.e. crowns) to keep all her teeth!

Edna was not easy to work on. She was lovely in every way except, she wouldn't let me treat her lying back. She had to be vertical because, "I get dizzy when lying so far back." I tried of course to adapt to her request. When treating her upper molars, I performed in a dental gymnastic position, known as the "total corkscrew." After working on her for any length of time, my back muscles would go into spasm. Deep down I knew the reason she wouldn't let me tip her back; she feared her wig falling off. I'd implore, "I must tip you back a drop." After a while, she'd relent and let me. She liked that I quickly placed my left forearm (I'm right handed) on the top of her head, and firmly pressed her wig to her head. This insured, her hairpiece wouldn't fall off. I dreaded every appointment!

Then unfortunately senility set in, for both Beckers. As time went on their appearances became unkempt, and it was obvious their dental hygiene was sorely lacking. This led to more and more dental work. Now I had to spend more time on Mr. Becker, as he was deteriorating faster. Bob also insisted on keeping all of his teeth. Due to the aforementioned circumstances, I spent an inordinate amount of time working on them, in the never ending battle against tooth decay. Knowing I couldn't keep up with the onslaughts of dementia and acid reflux, I faced a conundrum that wasn't taught in dental school. This was an ethical dilemma. How much time, effort and money should one invest in a no-win situation? Again, they were adamant in their desire to keep their teeth.

One day after seeing Mrs. Becker and then my chiropractor, I made a momentous decision. Mrs. Becker had a large cavity on her upper last tooth. (wisdom tooth) As you know, most patients have their wisdom teeth removed at an early age. I announced to Mrs. Becker, "Your wisdom tooth must come out." After an impassioned discussion, the Beckers agreed. We got the consent of her physician (because of blood thinners) and stopped her medication for a week. This would reduce the amount of bleeding during and after her extraction.

Edna wanted me to remove the wisdom tooth because she was most comfortable with me, and didn't want to see an oral surgeon. However unbeknownst to all, the X-rays didn't show, this tooth was fused to the jawbone. As a result, some of the bone came out with the tooth. Even though she had stopped taking her blood thinners, there was considerably more bleeding than expected. Profusely, might be the better word to describe the scene. My first thought after some deliberation, was to find my sneakers and run. Inherently knowing this would be inappropriate, I had to now thoroughly suture the site, to stem the outpour. Since it could have been a life threatening event, I insisted, "We have to lean you back all the way!" Of course, the wig hit the floor and I inadvertently stepped on it. Fortunately, the blond wig wasn't transformed into making Mrs. Becker a red head. The bleeding ceased after I placed about fifty stitches. I even thought of suturing her tongue near her cheek to stop the bleeding, but that was strictly tongue in cheek. After what seemed like an hour, I finally got her under control. After we were sure she was under control we scheduled a post-surgical visit.

For a decade I treated this great couple. Every two weeks, at least one of them was in my office having work. As an aside, we had an extension added to our house, as a result of their numerous visits. Appropriately, we named it the "Becker Wing." My wife and I did entertain them there and they loved that we named this section of our house after them.

Eventually, they moved to an assisted living facility, and since passed. I'm sure the tooth fairies up there, are putting forth the very same valiant effort that I gave them.

A WRY DRY RUN

My wife, Iris and I purchased tickets to Manhattan at a LIRR station, holding our suitcase and large shopping bag that had the Hospital for Special Surgery (HSS) logo. Two strangers asked if I was having surgery there. Both paid tribute to the splendor of the hospital. I was having hip replacement there, and comforted by their positive words.

We went in the day before and stayed at the Helmsley Medical Tower, which is next to and affiliated with the hospital. This accommodation helped ease the trek from eastern Long Island for my 6:00AM surgery. Going to the city before surgery, presented totally mixed signals to our psyches. Whenever we traveled to NYC, it was always for fun or entertainment. Never before was there angst and fear going to the "Big Apple." The hotel room was spacious and quite reasonable. HSS gives you a discount on your "surgical NYC get away." Getting ready for the operation, the idea of an escape does cross your mind. The hospital is located in the E. 70's, and beautifully hugs the East River. It is a gorgeous setting and rivals any European river vista.

Entering the hospital, I was treated like a special guest in a

National Park hotel. I was ushered into an atrium that overlooked this stunning waterway. Regularly you'd see all types of boats – commerce, speed and sail. These vessels matched the diversified interests of New Yorkers.

Surprisingly, HSS had many patients who looked like my relatives. Everyone had the same exact gait as my mother, sisters and me, as they teetered about the reception area. My family also has a history of Alzheimer's. Everyone at the hospital, from physicians to auxiliaries painstakingly asked my name and date of birth. For a moment, I thought it was a ploy of my wife to sign me into an Alzheimer's unit!

My cardiologist and orthopedist chose general anesthesia instead of epidural for my hip surgery. Before the procedure, Dr. M. Farley literally initialed my right hip with a huge "MF." Growing up in Brooklyn and having a street vernacular, I smiled when I saw these letters. Being of sane mind, I didn't dare tell him what the letters implied to me. Soon thereafter, a young lady anesthesiologist introduced herself. Not being very professional, she announced to me and my family, "In my judgment, surgery (scheduled in ten minutes) would be best accomplished by using epidural anesthesia." This would then postpone the impending surgery three days, because of my taking blood thinners. Re-entering the room, Dr. Farley was informed of her opinions and forcefully told the anesthesiologist, "This was already discussed with his cardiologist and general anesthesia is the modality." After this upsetting encounter, I was wheeled into the operating room. My wife and son were informed the ensuing surgery would be about two hours.

Now I want to impress the reader with the importance of having a second person accompanying the spouse, parent, or whoever of the patient. Thirty minutes into the operation, the surgeon came into the waiting room looking for my wife. At that moment, Iris thought she was single again. He said, "He's fine, but we had to stop the surgery because his blood pressure was too low."

Recently after being dehydrated, I had passed out a couple of times. My cardiologist implanted a pacemaker, to help obviate this problem. The anesthesiologist not being experienced opted to play it safe and didn't wait the appropriate time for this particular pacemaker to kick in. (In retrospect, who knows, maybe there was a life threatening problem. If so, a ghostwriter would have completed this story.) My wife worried who was going to tell me, "No surgery took place." When I awoke, still stupefied from the anesthesia, a nurse revealed what happened. My first impression was this nurse had a great sense of humor. It was something I might have joked, to a friend or relative. I was sure I was dreaming. I wasn't! Immediately, the surgical team called a technician to test my pacemaker's accuracy. With the anesthesiologist present, the expert assured everyone, it operated perfectly.

A few days later, after a new battery of tests, the group was satisfied that I could reschedule my surgery. I emphatically told my orthopedist, "I'd like a different anesthesiologist. Pick someone you're comfortable with, and please try do this ASAP." This time, they stopped my blood thinners and performed the operation using epidural anesthesia. Getting really pumped up for surgery and then having the gas taken out, was a downer.

My close contacts know I love to practice and be prepared. However, this dress (actually I was undressed) rehearsal was overkill. The surgery was rescheduled in five days and for my wife and me, it was *déjà vu*. Forebodingly, the night before the second surgery, there was a fire at our hotel and four fire trucks responded.

HSS brought in two seasoned "gas passers." (In medical lexicon, a moniker for an anesthesiologist is gas passer.) The senior anesthesiologist had both MD and Ph.D. degrees. Prior to surgery, they requested a technician from the pacemaker company, to change some settings. Dr. Mark Farley re-initialed the area. I bantered, "I have a photo of your initials, from the first time. I could put it on EBay and make some money." He retorted "It wouldn't be worth very much." He then asked as the minutes ticked off, "Are you uptight?" I replied in front of my family, "I get more uptight before a golf outing." He answered, "In that case, you shouldn't be playing golf." I did eventually follow my doctor's orders.

June 21st the longest day of the year, also the date of my surgery went on forever. All the experts had assembled, except the technician, who arrived half-hour late because of traffic. The technician connected his computer to my pacemaker to ensure it worked properly. Lying on the gurney, in front of the medical team, he set my heart rate on high. I felt like I was running a 440-yard dash, without moving a muscle. Talk about an out of body experience! Not a bad way to lose weight either.

The surgery went flawlessly and I awoke in the recovery room feeling terrific. The entire medical team was absolutely great. At this renowned teaching hospital, every race, color, and nationality was represented. Somehow, these diverse health care workers all speak a universal language. The attitude and intelligence of these prideful health care professionals resonates throughout HSS.

Twenty-four hours after surgery, they had me moving with a walker. It was easy! I had an IV narcotic cocktail administered continuously. Feeling no pain, and since I love to show off, I flew around the recovery area. An assistant pulled me aside and said, "SLOW Down!" She warned, "If they see you're doing too well, they won't put you in a rehab facility." The aide whispered, "The government has stool pigeons, take it easy, take it easy."

I now walked taller than in years. The average person loses one-half an inch in their lifetime. I come from a long line of shrinkers and already lost about two inches to date. My maximum height was 6 feet and going at the present rate, I thought I'd be

5 feet 7 in. at my sayonara. Since I'm having my knee done, the surgeon thought he could restore some of my height. I of course, asked for four inches, but we settled on one.

I did follow my aide's advice, slowed my walker and passed the conditions for rehab. I was transported to St. Charles Rehabilitation in Port Jefferson by ambulance. First time in an ambulance and I had to lie on a stretcher, facing backwards. Disturbingly, I reflected I might have only one more similar ride like this left. The ride/word, rhymes with the word curse! - I felt every pothole, as they reverberated throughout my body. Not knowing when the next rut is coming, every pothole became magnified.

I mused about going to St. Charles for "triple rehabilitation." Hip replacement therapy was obvious. Secondly, everyone thinks they'll get addicted to the tons of narcotics given for pain. Thirdly, after my day at work, I'd always look forward to an alcoholic drink, to relax and unwind. It was now ten days since I had my last alcohol. Obviously, it didn't matter what floor they'd dropped me off, as I was sure, I'd need "rehab while rehabbing."

At St. Charles Hospital, I wasn't familiar with the many religious icons and their Morning Prayers. One day a Caribbean looking pastor (An Idi Amin clone) dressed in vivid regalia, asked if I'd be interested in a healing prayer. I stated "I was raised Jewish but I'm not religious." Immediately, he took out his prayer book and preached non-stop. My roommate couldn't handle it. He told the pastor, "I'm an agnostic and find you repugnant!" He told the peacock-attired minister, "Get the hell out of here!"

My roommate had knee replacement and was also on heavy duty narcotics. For those who don't know, these analgesics cause awful constipation. We were together for a week. He had his PhD in economics and also had a warped sense of humor. As a result, I named our personal commode the "virgin toilet seat."

Hip, hip, hooray, one surgery down and now planning my

knee replacement. However, I think I'll give it some time before I book it. This way it'll give my writings a reprieve for a while.

"Age is the reluctant march into enemy territory."

William James

POSITIONS IN BED

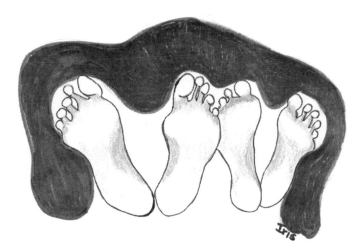

"Get away from me, you're getting too close!" my wife Iris screamed. Iris and I recently had orthopedic surgeries that impacted on our sleep. Picture our bed. (I know that might be upsetting.) If one is facing our bed, she sleeps on the right side and I sleep on the left. Recently, I had my left knee replaced and she had her right foot operated on. If either one barely touched the other's surgerized region, there was intense pain, and usually outbursts of expletives.

Therefore, I suggested while recuperating, it would be beneficial if we changed sides or sleep in separate rooms.

The thought of sleeping and waking on the "wrong side of the bed" is fraught with confusion and angst. Not being in your customary position, usually results in wakening disoriented and not sleeping as well.

Last week we went to dinner with two other couples, both of whom have been married forty years. My wife and I really didn't know this foursome well. After a few tongue loosening drinks, I segued the conversation into "let's talk about positions in bed." (You should have seen their faces! - I even paused for a while, to increase the dramatic effect, then told them where I was going.) One couple chose their sides by emulating how their parents slept. Unfortunately, this couple both wanted the same side of the bed and fought over it. My wife and I consciously chose the handedness concept. Since she's lefty and I'm righty, it was a no brainer for her to sleep on the right side, while she appreciates my dominant hand on the left side of the bed. It's easier to shut the alarm clock, pick up the phone, or do the other things if your main hand does the work.

Sex in theory, should be better if the partners have different handedness and sleep on the correct sides. You will have to envision some bedroom spatial relationships, to know I am correct. Since we all have a higher degree of dexterity in our dominant hand, we should be able to do a better job in these "behind closed doors activities." Incidentally, the percentage of lefties in the world is somewhere around ten to thirteen. One of the men at this dinner was a Math teacher, who figured on the spot, the probability of having an ideal match up of one righty and lefty is between twenty and twenty-three percent.

Folklores abound as to how you pick the side of the bed you sleep, including the "caveman mentality." The husband sleeps closest to the door in the chivalrous concept of being the defender, in case there's an intruder. A woman might pick the side closest to the door, because she's the one who gets up during the night to nurse. In most families, the mother is the lighter sleeper and can attend to the child more quickly, if he's sick or has a nightmare. The woman also is usually more compassionate in the middle of the night.

A psychological theory suggests, when a bed is against a wall, the man subconsciously "traps" the woman by not letting her out without his permission. Another factor that could influence the side is the position you slept before you joined your partner, as in a previous relationship. The temperature source (heating or air conditioning) may also factor in, if one mate has an internal thermostat issue.

Other dynamics that could mess with your sleeping arrangements may include – the television being too low, and/or a guy with clown feet. Installing a TV wall mount or selecting a man with smaller feet, always helps in these situations. Astonishingly, I even heard of one couple who have no preferences, and sleep on whichever side, whenever! As an aside, twenty percent of couples sleep in different bedrooms, whatever that means.

Later in life, sometimes one spouse develops a disability and must be closer to the bathroom. Depending on the distance to the lavatory and the propensity of using "Depends" – changing positions is usually a very hard habit to break. Changing "Depends" is not pleasant either.

It's always interesting to see what transpires when a couple goes to a motel and has to select their side. In general there are no steadfast rules. Usually they take the same sides as they normally do, but not always. However, the concepts of caveman, children, closest to the bathroom again may factor in.

In finishing up these thoughts let's talk about second marriages and our final positions – burial plots. On second thought I'm getting a little tired and I'll get back to you on that. I'm off to my side of the bed.

A SHITTY RETIREMENT

My seventy-five year next door neighbor Harry greeted me as I drove into my driveway. He was in a rare, marvelous frame of mind and announced, "I just had a colonoscopy and I'm clean as a whistle." I thought to myself, he was still full of shit; even after his recent colonoscopy. He couldn't ever be happy or in a good mood!

When I think of Harry, I picture him walking his four dogs. How can anyone not be depressed, picking up feces of four dogs – every day, sometimes twice a day? The thought of being involved with a pooper scooper, a substantial portion of the day is repulsive. Additionally, Harry is a victim of constant turd tension; always imploring his dogs to defecate.

Not only is Harry tethered to his dogs, he's also tied to his wife. It's sad watching him kowtow to everything she demands. He really is a total wuss. She barks, growls and chews him out, every time he's in earshot. The so called "top dog" is a down trodden wimp who "shits a brick" whenever he's in her company.

As a result of his cleaning up fecal matter and taking these verbal abuses, depressed Harry must feel he's on the lowest rung of society. Harry is also totally isolated, which contributes to his low opinion of himself. He walks around looking rear-ended by life, and sidesteps any eye contact while doing his doody.

Harry has become crapulent (excessive drinking) to combat his loss of self-esteem and get him through the day. Through the grapevine, I heard these neighbors are struggling financially. He really hit a low point in life and I truly feel sorry for him. I suggested an entre-manurial endeavor that might pick him up from being down in the dumps. Given that he's already shoveling, why not develop a business of helping others, pick up their pet feces. This business proposal actually brought a glimmer to his liquored eyes.

I pondered, "The only possible down side to this stinking business is scooper's elbow, especially after heavy rains, when the feces become soaked. Maybe you could explore a shitty contraption to tackle this problem. Perhaps, double gloving and putting peppermint under your nose might help the other issues."

Harry was flying high from my scatological suggestions. He recognized there was hope. He couldn't wait to unload this, on his wife. I even suggested this advertising slogan specifically suited for Harry's new endeavor: "I'm #1 with your dog's #2."

Thinking if this business goes, I could sincerely greet Harry every day with –

"Have a crappy day!

KRAMERS

Michael Kramer entered my life in the third grade, although he swears it was the fourth, and stayed. We'd invariably get the same test scores and therefore assumed whatever field one of us chose, the other could have selected the same line of work. Kramer however hated blood. Kramer, the most conservative of my friends, had a captivating spectacular laugh. Michael and I skipped a year in junior high. These accelerated classes had extremely bright students and we were the dumbest in our class. Nevertheless, we had a ball in school as we stumbled through our adolescent awakenings.

Mrs. Soloway, a no nonsense science teacher, taught sex education. This subject never had been taught in a junior high coed class at our Brooklyn school. The first class started with a movie and we were thoroughly warned if there were any shenanigans, we'd be sent to the principal. Being tall, we sat in the back, in front of the biggest, baddest dude Ben Mittler. Behind his back we called him "Froggy", because he looked like one. As the lights dimmed, we eagerly awaited the film. Froggy held a "Bic" pen that rested on his lower lip that leaked. By chance, Kramer turned and noticed a large blob of wet blue ink on his lip. Kramer poked me and said, "Look at Froggy." A second later, Froggy taps Kramer and grovels softly, "What's so funny?" Kramer without hesitating, "You got some ink on your cheek." Froggy took his finger (after touching the blob on his lip) and smeared his cheek as Kramer watched. Mike tapped me again, "Look again." I did, and chuckled. This started another round of Froggy tapping Kramer, asking "What's so funny?" This time he whispered, "You now got ink on your other cheek." Within five minutes Kramer painted and speckled Froggy's entire face with blobs and blobs of blue ink! All over! Trying to hide our laughter, we laughed even harder. I literally pissed in my pants. Suddenly Mrs. Soloway put the lights on shrieking, "Didn't I warn you there'd be no monkey business! The three of you, go to the principal." I was mortally embarrassed and still remember my junior high classmates pointing, as I walked cross-legged, trying to hide my very obvious "leakage." Kramer looked at me, then Froggy and then looked at both of us again. He absolutely exploded and howled with laugher! I guess this episode contributed to my feelings of inadequacy in sex education.

After school, we hung out at Kramer's private house. All my friends and I lived in typical Brooklyn six story apartments. Mrs. Kramer's had a great sense of humor and an unusual laugh. Behind her back, we called her Izzy, short for Isabel. Izzy often cornered me and asked, "How's Michael doing with the girls?" I'd invariably play with her, making up some outrageous half-truths. She was extremely gullible and dying to hear about her son. I'd concoct, "You know Diane Hirsch, the one who reached puberty, thinks he's adorable! I'm not supposed to tell you, but she asked him over Saturday. She told him her mother won't be home." I told Izzy, "I'm a little worried." Kramer would always get paranoid when I talked to his mother, as he knew of my outlandish stories. He'd actually run with breakneck speed, from wherever, to break up our chitchats. Mrs. Kramer incidentally, was on the heavy side and I treasured making her laugh. I loved watching Izzy's fat arms shake, and jiggle like Jell-O whenever I got her going.

Izzy was a perfect audience. She was motherly, warm, loved to listen, and had that body laugh. Izzy was also funny looking. She had a large nose that veered sharply to her right and a "long in the tooth" smile. Her teeth severely overlapped and leaned toward her left. Between her nose going one way and her slanted teeth the other, you weren't sure which side of her face to talk to. Izzy was embarrassed by her smile, and always placed her hand over her mouth when she laughed, which was often. She never fixed her teeth because she feared dentistry. I loved telling her I was going to be a dentist and watch her squirm.

Kramer and I had a brilliant routine we performed on classmates that could have won an Academy Award. After a significant test i.e. final or Regents, we'd corner a friend and small talk. I'd sigh in relief and say, "Glad this monster test was over." Kramer would ask, "How'd you do on the map questions?" The friend became crestfallen and shrieked, "What map question?" (there were none) I'd go along saying, "That was impossible! I put down Russia, Japan and Korea." Kramer rejoined "Russia was right, but I went with China and Hong Kong." We'd then argue. The color of our friend's face would completely drain; as we watched his knees slowly buckle!

Forty years ago my wife fixed up Kramer with her friend Dede, who became his wife. When the internet started, Dede was fascinated with the shopping and email features. Unexpectedly, I helped DD pick her email address. I suggested a perfect name, one that everyone would remember, ***DoubledDee@ aol.com.*** DD who is naïve loved it. Kramer smirked and went along with the prank. ***DoubleDee@aol*** lasted only a short time, as Double D was bombarded with more hits than anyone could imagine!

In the 1990's Seinfeld was the number one TV comedy. The character I loved most was Kramer. I couldn't take my eyes off him, with his famous entrances and pratfalls. To this day I'm still riveted by him. I became a dentist and have talked about my love affairs with "Kramers." Kim, a long term patient came to my office with a toothache. In the past Kim told me she was also enamored with Kramer on TV. Since Kim was in her first trimester and with first child, she wondered if it was OK to have dental procedures. I reassured her and said, "Just in case, call your obstetrician. Who's your doctor?" She said, "Dr. Kramer in Port Jefferson, but I call him Kramer, because of the Seinfeld show." I smiled and related, "Ironically, Dr. Kramer happens to be my distant cousin."

That night Kim went to dinner with her husband (also a delightful patient) and another couple. The other wife was also pregnant and used the same obstetrician, Dr. Kramer. In the past, Kim's husband had seen me clown around, while treating him. Kim told the other three, "You won't believe it, but Salmonson is Kramer's cousin." (meaning Dr. Kramer, the MD). Kim's husband thinking differently, (thought his wife meant their DDS is related to Seinfeld's Kramer) blurted, "You know, I could easily see them being related." Obviously, I absolutely loved Kim's husband seeing similarities between the comedian and me.

The Kramers, Salmonsons and the (third musketeer) Harrisons celebrate our five year birthdays by vacationing together. This past year our 65th was spent in New Orleans. Kramer has been a part of my life for sixty years. The name always brings a big smile to my face.

THOUGHTS BEFORE SURGERIES

Every age has its own unique set of joys and problems. What makes life exciting is that we've never traveled this path before. Therefore, there's always newness in the events that unfold. I've always approached life from a humorous viewpoint and that has helped me through the tough times.

I just received my Medicare card and like any card, I couldn't wait to use it. I feel like a "kid in a candy store." (Hospitals acting as stores and doctors as merchants) I've taken a crash course in a variety of medical problems that befits my being an *Alta Cocker.* I have a very noticeable limp and function in moderate pain. Previous exams have primed me for hip and knee replacement surgeries. I also had a few minor procedures with my cardiologist. The definition of a minor procedure, as we all know is – "When the procedure is done on someone else."

My last orthopedist exam was of interest. After he read my X-rays, I asked "What do you recommend and in what order?" He simply stated, "First the right hip, next the left knee and then the left hip." Driving home from the appointment, I almost had an alcohol related car accident. Not that I had a drink as yet, but I drove home as fast as I could, to down that martini or two.

I've always been precocious in every phase of life. I've grown up very fast, approached puberty earlier than most, married young and had kids and grandchildren before the majority of friends. Now it's only fitting, my body is older than nearly all my peers. On the flip side of leading the league in aging, I'm now guiding my friends in how to use Medicare.

My occupation is in the health care sector. I've interacted with hundreds of physicians, dentists, nurses etc. Benefitting by this lifelong network, I've created my own maxim "Cultivate as many health professionals as possible." This practical adage also helps friends and relatives, who've joined me in being part of what I call the "Breakdown Generation."

Arlene, my older sister, recently retired and was looking to do charity work. Unfortunately, she has the same cesspool of genes as me, and sees lots of doctors. Not being entirely altruistic, and contemplating both our future needs, I suggested volunteering in a hospital. Arlene took my advice and now works in a gift shop. She gets an employee discount that's valid in any NYC hospital. Since I'm on deck for a number of hospital procedures and appreciate visitors, I'll tell friends "Use my sister's discount before visiting me!" This way I'll have reading material and they'll save a few pennies. Additionally, her volunteering will benefit our medical networking, by connecting with other health providers. By the way, we'll gladly share our list of health professionals.

Hospitals in their grand design are notorious for the worst tasting food. I'm sure this is to discourage anyone from sticking around for their cuisine. You never heard of anyone gaining weight at a hospital. Since I'll be having a number of surgeries, I hope I don't have the opposite problem of losing too much weight. (Should hospitals advertise as diet centers, as a secondary benefit?)

My daughter-in-law has her PhD in coupons. She can purchase bags of groceries and pay little. Using her expertise, I asked her to be on the lookout for hospital coupons. (I'm sure with the overall population aging, they'll be coming.) This marketing tactic will be great for my peers, who are next in line for surgery.

One of my patients is a tattoo artist. We all know women who get permanent tattoos for eyebrows or lips. I asked, "Could you do a wrist tattoo that replicates a hospital wrist band?" This would save me considerable time being admitted.

In retirement I always wanted to travel. Now before boarding, I'll have to allow a lot more time at airports. I remember as a kid, we sang a song in assembly called "I Often Go a Wandering." Now I'll change the meaning of this song, to imply the slow process of having a wand placed over my knees, hips, etc. Visualizing this, I picture myself singing and slowly dancing in a pirouette, as I'm being wanded. (No such word as yet.)

I dedicate these muses to my fellow Breakdown Generationers, who by living longer are helping our economy increase our Gross National Medical Product.

BUYING A CHURCH

In my forty-plus years of dentistry I've done only one extraction
without anesthesia. My first dental office was a home office on
eastern Long Island. One Friday night just before sundown, and
after my last patient, Father Tartaglia from St. Mark's, walked in
unscheduled. He was in excruciating pain, holding his jaw, and
paced in the waiting room. From his past dental history, I knew

he was severely allergic to all forms of "Novocaine." It was the early'70's, and ironically, Father was in his early 70's also. I was five years out of school, two of which had been in the Army. I had done hundreds of extractions, as we tried to ensure there'd be fewer toothaches in Vietnam.

Absurdly, I had just cemented a crown on my own father, who happened to be my last patient of the day. It was Friday night as I mentioned, and my Dad was also on Long Island to attend synagogue (shul), with my son and me. We're not religious, but my twelve year old was preparing for his Bar Mitzvah, and we were required to attend services. After finishing up, our plans for the three of us were, eat and go to temple for Friday night services.

I told my father about Father's toothache. I was reluctant and apprehensive treating the priest due to the possibility of complications, again without anesthesia and the late hour. The dental specialists would be gone for the day! (In addition, our threesome had to be on time for services.) With the encouragement of my father, I made the decision to help Father. Tension mounted as we prepared for his treatment. Thankfully, given that it was after work, no other patients were present. My assistant called the priest in and placed the bib. Father made the sign of the cross at least twice. I had never seen anyone do the sign of the cross so earnestly before.

I then gave Father Tartaglia nitrous oxide (laughing gas) to calm him down. Just as importantly, to calm myself down! I asked, "Have you ever been called a High Priest before?" Father Tartaglia disclosed, "I have a tough time going to the dentist. Not only because I'm allergic to Novocaine but, I feel guilty and don't go, unless there's an emergency." I retorted, "I never thought I'd see the day, I'd take confession, and from a priest no less!" He chuckled and asked, "Are you religious?" I answered "No, but I was brought up Jewish and by chance, we're going to synagogue tonight, because my son is preparing for his Bar Mitzvah." Father Tartaglia seemed interested in this rite of passage. After that, we all prayed for obvious reasons; my assistant, because it was late and she wanted to get the hell out, Father because of his pain, and myself because of my commitment to my son. With the laughing gas flowing I said, "Since I'm later going to synagogue, this is the first time in my life I've ever "preprayed." I then asked Father, "Have you heard the line, all religions are the same; religion is basically guilt, with different holidays?"

I then drilled the tooth to see if it was salvageable. Father Tartaglia now buzzed said, "I've been to the dentist many times, so I know the drill, but somehow I still get a chill." His bicuspid, the root of his problem, was indeed hopeless and had to be extracted. During the next few moments, which felt like eternity, I'm not sure who perspired more Father or this dentist. A Supernatural being surely intervened, as the tooth flew out! Father immediately said a "Hail Mary." I was now schooled in the "Hail Mary", and soon off to shul.

A week later, Father Tartaglia returned to thank me, and requested a private talk. I had no idea what he wanted, and of course thought maybe I'm in trouble with God. (God forbid) At our meeting, he told of his epiphany. "Our hundred year old St. Mark's church can't accommodate its constituents any more. We're building a new church and the old one is for sale. I heard through the grapevine, you've outgrown your home office. I thought our church would be a great location for your dental office." I of course, loved the concept of a Jewish guy from Brooklyn, buying a church. I couldn't wait to tell my friends and family. I didn't know anyone in my religion, who bought a church! It seemed like an unusual divination, the timing impeccable.

There were many problems changing the church into a dental office. The foundation had to be redone. We contracted a house mover to lift the building, while a new foundation was poured.

The church never even had a bathroom, solely an outhouse. This building actually predated zoning codes! It took two years to complete the renovation. Finally it was done – Thanks to you know who.

Some worshippers' families had been parishioners four generations and eagerly awaited the transformation. Many families had their baptisms, communions, confirmations, weddings and funeral masses at this holy site. Often, these rituals were where their greatest family bonds occurred. I hoped to continue with their bondings.

Original pews were given away to patients who requested them. Some people who weren't patients, changed to our office because of the sacredness of the building. Yes, they thought their dental work would be blessed.

People who were prior church members and now patients were asked, "Where would you like to sit?" As you may know, church-goers like to sit in their usual places. After they were seated, and before their dental work, I would put my hand on their shoulder and solemnly say "Let us pray!" Dentists invariably control conversations and sermonize on many topics during dental work. After treatment, I would turn off the overhead light and sometimes ask "Did you see the light?"

Nitrous oxide (laughing gas) can elicit confession like responses from some patients. However, I've never considered asking for donations for these rituals. I've been known to talk about their "pearly whites" and sometimes segue to the "pearly gates." Some patients, the Popes (Herb and Judy), have been with me, for what seems like eternity.

In this office, there's been a continuity of service, as my son has taken over the practice. Because of this, we can talk about the Father, Son and .... Hmm. Has this dentist been affected by the "Bats in the Belfry?"

The "church" has been mutually beneficial to this Jewish guy, his family and in addition, caringly serves the community. We've also preserved an historic landmark that's over hundred years old. I am now thinking about buying another. I wonder – is St. Patrick's available?

I AM MY MOTHER

Whenever my wife wants to get my goat she'll say, "You're getting to be more and more like your mother." Of course she'd be using it in the pejorative, in that it always has a derogatory or less than pleasant connotation. It always gets my ire fomenting. Unfortunately as I now have more time to reflect, I have come to the conclusion my wife is probably right.

People who knew my mother (Dorothy, deceased twenty

years) often point out our similarities. We both have (had) a healthy looking florid complexion. This genetic coloration comes from high blood pressure and a skin condition called rosacea. This imparts a so called healthy redness and very little wrinkles, while in fact it's harmful.

Not proudly, I've always had an issue with sweating. As a kid, I led the league, with the largest armpit perspiration rings ever documented. On a good or bad day, depending on your definition, they'd actually meet in the middle of my shirt. I'd tell people, "I bought the shirt prestained from Macy's." Playing tennis, my opponents wouldn't allow me to put the tennis balls into my pants' pockets, because they'd get too soggy and slow the game. I got this from Dottie - always hot. We both wore overcoats in the winter, just to appear normal. My mother loved to visit me at the Univ. of Buffalo, (she championed my decision to go there) because of her negative thermotropism. (movement away from heat) As she got older, she sweated or worried about everything. Now semi-retired in Florida, I sweat and fret big time like her.

My mother had a love affair with hats. Mom didn't have good hair. It was reddish (depending on her age) quite curly and much thinner than most women. Since it often got wet (from perspiration), hats were a natural segue. I have male pattern baldness or is it female pattern baldness (my father had thick hair), and similarly love caps. (dental caps also) As an aside, she had "a thing" about teeth and was crazy about her dentist. She pushed dentistry as my career path and eventually I led my son down this same road. (dental genes?)

Dottie had a very good sense of humor. What made her stand out was her spectacular laugh. Literally, before the advent of canned laughter, she could've been hired by any movie theater, play, or TV show to bring down the house. Once she got going, she couldn't stop! People would stop whatever they were doing, to listen. It was seriously contagious! As a kid, I'd do just about anything to make her laugh. I'm sure subconsciously, hearing her laugh greatly influenced my gravitation towards humor.

As Mom aged, she developed a peculiar walk, from her "bad hip" as she called it. Her gait had a pronounced wobble, stutter and teeter. It took her a while to get going from a sitting position. She also had trouble tying her shoes. These features I learned are characteristic of someone needing hip replacement. My walk now is the same as hers. In the past, I assumed my athletic participation, which took its toll over the years, was the reason for my hip and knee problems. My mother, who had the same walk as I said, had zero interest in sports. She was a good dancer however, with the Charleston, being her favorite. I'm sure she passed on this gene to me, as I also love the dance floor. Musing over our joint problems, I'm convinced having a genetic predisposition to arthritis was the main culprit in our breakdowns. We both are replete with arthritis. Nevertheless, I still like to think, athletics aggravated my plight. In addition, my plump mother and her puffy son's expertise in using our forks never helped the loads on our joints.

Whether because of her "bad hip," too much weight, being a drop lazy, or a combination of the above, Dotty had a PhD in "while you're up." She was a master of asking anyone, while they're up, to get something for her. If you didn't know her act, she could win an Academy Award. She would do it seamlessly. Of course, now that I'm struggling with my own joint problems, I've had the benefit of being taught by the master. Unfortunately, I'm not nearly as good as she was, as yet.

Dotty repeated her stories over and over to anyone in earshot. She had no knowledge or better yet, didn't seem to care that she repeated herself. In all her stories, she rambled on .... into ridiculous minutia. After a while, anyone who listened would get that far away, glassy look in their eyes. You'd pretend to listen, and hope not to get caught. Not proudly, I see this same look on people's faces, when I go into one of my many diatribes.

Since Dorothy was a child of the depression, she learned early on to be extremely frugal. In restaurants, "doggy bagging" was her forte. First, she took leftovers and rolls. I always sweated her overstuffed pocketbook would explode. If there was **any** room left, she'd take - packets of sugar, salt, pepper, and Sweet and Low. She'd take anything not nailed down. Now in my old age, some of these items are starting to look very, very tempting. After all, your mother's always right!

At this moment, I'd like to tell you two more very private things, but keep it to yourself. Don't tell another soul. The space between my front teeth is getting bigger (like Mom's) and now my breasts are bigger than they've ever been.

Therefore, since I'm always flushed and now have a bust, keep it hushed – I'm becoming my mother.

CAMEL CROTCH

While on a two week Israeli bus tour, with my wife and another couple, we took a camel ride. Technically, it was a dromedary. (one hump, camel has two) Getting on and off and the actual ride was a pre-chiropractic experience. Unlike horses, camels kneel down to pick up their passengers and cargo. As they stand, your body is simultaneously going in so many directions that you feel like you're on a bucking bronco. (Not surprisingly, I've never been on one of those as yet.) This thousand pound animal, herky - jerked me for about a mile. I walked the camel for a mile, rather than walk a mile for a camel.

Nevertheless, I couldn't wait to get off the smelly creature because of burning and soreness in my groin area. The local villagers charged $20 for the ride, which I thought was quite fair. However, when disembarking from the camel, the Arabs said, "That'll be $100 to get off the camel." Shocked and scared out of our minds, we were being held hostage. With no feasible options, we trembled as we handed over the cash.

After this body and now mind boggling experience, it took hours to calm down. I still however, needed an ointment for my severe case of camel crotch. Recovering from this harrowing episode, I searched the desert in vain, for Israeli Desitin. I was somewhat pacified by the fact, the next day of our Muddled East tour, we'd be going to the Dead Sea. It's well known for its much needed pampering and curative therapies. The tour guide ominously warned however, "You shouldn't swim in the Dead Sea if you have any open wounds, nicks, or cuts - both inside and out. Also, don't shave the day you go. If any Dead Sea water gets into your eyes or mucous membranes, it'll cause tremendous burning and pain."

The Dead Sea is the lowest point on earth (1,300 ft. below sea level) and has the opposite effect of going to a high altitude area. Everyone knows breathing in the Mile High City of Denver is hard because one often feels light headed due to the diminished oxygen. The Dead Sea has the opposite effect. The atmosphere is supersaturated with oxygen and people often feel "high" from this phenomenon. I guess you can say, "They feel high when they're so low." The Dead Sea is 33% salt and nothing lives. The Atlantic and Pacific Oceans have about a 3% salt content. Initially, salt burns any wound intensely, and after a while, it has great healing capacity. People with various skin and health maladies go there for its recuperative powers and stay for months.

After careful deliberation, evaluating my camel crotch rash and how my hemorrhoids were doing that day, I made the momentous decision to enter. Fear was omnipresent. I was the only member of our immediate group of four to enter. Not even my macho male friend, a retired football and baseball coach joined me. At first all were going, but the others pusillanimously chickened out.

I am sure the "high" from the increased levels of oxygen influenced my decision to go in. Not surprisingly, the **PAIN** made me think of one more reason why it's called the Dead Sea. People hope for death, from this lancet like agony. Fortunately, this pain lasted only three or four minutes; not nearly as long as I'd been forewarned.

Another reason I wanted to partake was, never in my life had I been able to float. Everyone said, "You'll be amazed how easily you float." Sure enough, I did so effortlessly. I floated so easily that I had some difficulty putting my legs down afterward, when I tried to stand. By the way, I have a great picture of myself floating in the Dead Sea and reading a newspaper.

Next was the ritual placement of "mud" all over my body for medicinal purposes. And I mean all over my body! Not a speck of skin showed. My friend who took photos of me as I applied the mud, couldn't stop laughing and snapping - laughing and snapping. I'll do just about anything for a great picture! All I could think about was that I looked like the old time singer Al Jolson. Of course, I did one or two of his songs, Swanee being my favorite.

My wife thoughtfully bought "Ahava" lotion at the Dead Sea Spa. It was a minerally enriched body salve for my camel crotch. It was carefully and liberally applied, and I did get the desired therapeutic and other benefits.

We felt quite safe the rest of the trip, though Israeli army troops with rifles seemed to be everywhere. The only incident occurred when we stayed on a kibbutz, a mile from Lebanon. A missile, possibly sent by the Hamas, soared by. I don't think they had any idea I was in the area, but that story might be my next one – or not.

TEMPERATURE TAKING SYNDROME

It all started with my nine year old granddaughter staying at our house when she was sick. Lauren had strep and missed four days of school with a high fever of 103.5F. She was on antibiotics and Tylenol, hoping her temperature would go down. She desperately wanted to feel better and resume her activities. Lauren took her temperature constantly, watching it rise and fall. She must have taken her temperature ten to twelve times a day. Every time she took it, Lauren tried to read the thermometer, and invariably became totally cross- eyed. This image could have conjured up a classic Norman Rockwell painting.

This temperature taking brought me back to my early childhood, when my mother took mine. Of course, when I was sick, it was in the early days of thermometers. Very few families had them, and they were taken rectally. This was most traumatic, as my mother was just learning the technique. My mother not being very dexterous, and not knowing anatomy, would insert it - come out - re-insert it - miss - numerous excruciating times. From these workouts, my gluteus muscles would get extremely tight. I'd involuntarily block these penetrations. Maybe from these events, that's why my wife and some close friends tell me I have a nice ass. In all likelihood from my mother's ineptness, I have absolutely no propensity towards homosexuality.

As she took my temperature, she'd invariably say "Hold still, do you want the glass thermometer to break?" Even at two or three years, I inherently knew I didn't want that glass device to break.

My mother was so proud she had the ability to read the thermometer! She'd tell my sister and me, it's difficult to do, and many of her friends and relatives hadn't been able to master this complicated skill. At the time, I believed everything my mother told me, and held her in mystical awe. Watching her read the thermometer, was a breath taking experience. (Because without the thing, in my you know what, I could breathe) After she withdrew the probe, she'd wipe it, close one eye, and very, very slowly, twirl it back and forth. She'd use her dramatic flair, as she paused, cleared her throat, and announced 102.8! I always waited with baited breath on the verdict. (Because I didn't want her to do it again!)

There was a special rule I'm sure Mom acquired from the doctor. You couldn't go to school, until your temperature was normal for 48 hours. Not enthralled with my mother's techniques, I dreaded each and every reading.

Let's fast forward to when I was eight or nine. My mother now was teaching my sister and me how to read the thermometer. I was fascinated as I watched the mercury dart, jump, and recede. I also learned how to read decimals. It looked like a sophisticated toy. One day when my mother wasn't around, my sister and I decided to play with it. As I was shaking it, like my mother did, I accidentally dropped it. The glass broke on the floor and the mercury stayed in this amorphous, self-contained glob. My mother heard the commotion, ran in and screamed louder than any mother you've ever heard, "Do you know how much that thermometer costs? – Just wait, just you wait til your father gets home!" Now I had to clean up the broken thermometer. It was completely mystifying, as I couldn't remove the mercury off the floor. It defied the laws of physics. Fascinating!

This mesmerizing movement of mercury, I think helped guide me into the field of dentistry. Years ago, in the making of silver fillings, the dentist would bring together mercury with a powdery mixture. This material hardened into the silver amalgam fillings that we know.

My granddaughter's obsession with taking her temperature reminded me of her father (my younger son) as a child. He also loved taking his temperature and did it repeatedly. My son however, took his orally, as technology had greatly improved. This son also became a dentist. Coincidentally, his daughter Lauren has shown an aptitude for working with her hands and has expressed an interest in dentistry.

I remember vividly telling my sons about the transition between taking your temperature rectally and orally. It was paradise; not having your mother, "Put that piece of glass up your ass."

The changeover from rectal to oral thermometers had some interesting side notes. When I was around eleven, we had both, in our medicine cabinet. Since the difference between the two, RECTAL and ORAL was only a few letters, you had to concentrate which you selected. My mother was now starting to need reading glasses and relied on her kids at times, to differentiate letters. When my older sister got sick, my mother asked me to get the oral thermometer. Depending on how pissed off I was at my sister, would influence my thermometer selection. Up until now, she never knew about this. Of course, **ALL** my friends in the **ENTIRE** neighborhood knew of my shenanigans. This led to one of the first jokes I ever created. "What's the difference between an oral and rectal thermometer? – The Taste!

I believe my son who has this temperature taking obsession,

acquired this fixation watching his mother (my wife) take her temperature. She takes it a zillion times, at the slightest impending malady. Incidentally, my wife is an artist and also has great manual dexterity.

I'm sure you've heard by now, dentists have the highest rate of suicide among all professionals. I have often wondered about this and why it's so. Whenever anyone asks me if I've ever thought about suicide, I invariably say, "No! Should I?"

I believe I've made effective inroads into a new theory and developed a hypothesis for further review. The "Temperature Taking Syndrome" may include the following characteristics –

1) Taking one's temperature often
2) Mercury fascination
3) Manual dexterity
4) Suicidal tendencies

Further study is necessary. I am sincerely requesting donations to fund this research. Please send your contributions to:

Ron Salmonson

SEE MORE OF SEYMOUR

Seymour Lukin, a friend of forty years has been my teacher. Some of the things he taught me - golf, cycling, kayaking, Chinese cooking, and driving a stick shift. He has also taught me a few things I can't write about. I believe the third most beloved word in the English language after mother and father, is teacher. A good teacher is a master of simplification, which he does with ease.

Sy ran a successful pesticide company on Long Island, aided by his Master's degree in business. However in midlife, he had an epiphany and returned to school to become a physics teacher. At Half Hollows East H.S. (a prestigious school on Long Island), he taught honors classes in this subject. Now retired, he still uses his knowledge of physics, i.e. driving a golf ball, cycling, and driving his wife crazy, (checking if I put you to sleep) as part of his everyday life.

During summers, he worked at a sleep away camp running the food service for over three hundred campers and staff. My wife and I entrusted Sy and his wife Tama to act as surrogate parents for our sons at this camp. When not involved with the camp's kitchen, C-more (Sy) taught our sons sailing and water skiing. They also helped our youngest when he was severely homesick. When asked what's best about teaching, Sy smiles and says, "July and August."

C-more is a total daredevil who still craves new adventures, whether it's a kayaking race to the Statue of Liberty, downhill skiing or mountain biking. Many of these activities require helmets. Consequently, his competitors never realize the vast difference in ages, until the competition is over. After he doffs his hat - the looks on his opponents' faces are priceless! – Often they're thirty years younger. For Sy's sixtieth birthday, his family gave him a gift certificate for trapeze school. The venue was in lower Manhattan and of course, he was the oldest by far. The next oldest was twenty-five. On the other hand, Sy leads the league in most visits to hospitals. He is well versed in broken bones and rehab programs. Although not evil, Sy and Evel Knievel might be genetically related.

Through his boundless energy, enthusiasm, and attitude, my friend became a revered instructor. Worthy of some Broadway productions, Sy's classroom presentations hammered home his physics lessons. To this day, C-more receives letters from students expressing their gratitude for his efforts and guidance. Teaching is a profession that teaches all other professions. I believe if you are fluent in a subject and have this gift, its incumbent to pass along your knowledge. Looking back, it's certainly difficult to gauge his immeasurable influence on the lives of his students.

In retirement, the Lukins bought an apartment in NYC. Always involved, he became president of this residential building. He presides over a nine hundred apartment complex, with a four million dollar annual budget. He has among many things, implemented an energy conversion system that saves its occupants a ton of money. Fortunately for its residents and sometimes unfortunately for Sy, it occupies a vast amount of his time.

The Lukins have their "PhDs" in taking advantage of Manhattan's culture. They're docents for "Open House New York", an annual architectural event. They also help ushering Off Broadway shows. In keeping with his true calling, Seymour volunteers at the mayor's office as a "Big Apple Greeter," guiding and educating tourists around Manhattan. His vigor and vitality imparts a "track meet" tempo for tourists to keep pace, as I can personally attest. (Sy took six of my friends on a five hour phenomenal, whirlwind excursion of lower New York.) Sy takes this very seriously; he's always learning new facts about the greatest city, which he conveys to his groups. Unfortunately with all these commitments, my wife and I C- less of C-more.

Growing up in Queens, Seymour was the only son of Holocaust survivors. He never knew about his biological father, who perished at Auschwitz, until he was introduced to unknown relatives at his *bar mitzvah*. (His mother remarried, when Sy was two and they raised him withholding this information.) Sy confessed, "This stunned and greatly impacted on my life. It sent me into an emotional free fall and took away the solid ground I walked on. I searched and searched to find my relatives in Europe and Canada."

Sy is upbeat with an exceptional sense of humor. He cares about people, and as you can see, certainly gets involved. Additionally, he's active in prostate cancer support groups (had it thirteen years ago) and keeps up with the literature. When asked, he's always there for advice.

If I needed any help, he'd be one of the first people I'd call. He would literally give you his pants, if asked. (Recently Sy did give me some of his pants, as he lost weight. Maybe that's why I like him so much. I got into his pants.) - I hoped you at least "syed" at that line!

My friend and teacher Sy has been a cherished gift and I sincerely express my thanks. Teachers are one of the most important members of society. Appropriately, the Talmud (A Jewish collection ironically of teachings) might have said it best:

"When you teach your son, you teach your son's son."

HAMSTRUNG BY MY HAMSTRINGS

The word hamstrung is derived from ancient warfare, when conquerors used their swords to slice the hamstring muscles of their crushed adversaries. This left the victims in unbelievable pain, incapacitated and immobile. "OUCH!!"

I am presently undergoing physical therapy for the zillionth time. Now it's my hamstring, which I tore playing tennis. In the last two years, I've been in therapy for hip and knee replacements, followed by ankle and Achilles injuries. My fatal flaw must be anything below my waist. I'm known in the physical therapy jargon as a "frequent flyer," which is a step up from their "frequent faller" classification. Their phone number, which I have on speed dial, is 1-800-THERAPIST.

After the first replacement surgery, my New York orthopedist authorized a handicapped parking sticker. The sticker has a five year time frame and at the time, I thought it was overkill. Maybe after he scrutinized the X-rays of my other joints, he knew my subsequent fate. Now wintering in Florida, everyone seems to have one. It's almost as if you don't have one there, there's something wrong with you.

Bill my physical therapist, who I now know on a first name basis, is quite knowledgeable with hamstring problems. Bill stated, "Every seven minutes someone pulls a hammie in aerobics class." I chuckled, "That's funny - the irony of people injuring themselves, trying to get healthy!"

My injury occurred playing doubles in an over fifty-five year old community. Over fifty-five means, I was playing with people who've also had over "fifty-five" previous injuries. I had strained this muscle two weeks before and came back too soon. This already tweaked muscle promptly tore. I had a huge black and blue hematoma that radiated down the back of my leg. I told everyone "My first tattoo." "You want to play? - One day you'll pay" is surely an appropriate adage. Unfortunately, injuries multiply with age and last longer. I certainly wouldn't take back the joys of participating in sports all my life, for now being a physical therapist's dream.

I was playing doubles and vividly remember the moment of disaster. There was a short ball and my partner yelled "Yours!" Never feeling like I'm on the wrong side of my seventh decade, I exploded for the ball, and immediately felt the "pop." I was sure someone shot me. I writhed in pain, hopped a few steps and then the ground said hello to me.

Everyone knows tennis is not a contact game. Surprisingly, there's more contact than you think. After all, you do have to contact the ball, and sometimes you contact the net or ground inadvertently, as was my case. In addition, contacting your physician sometimes does occur. However, never being the first to run to his doctor, I treated the injury myself. Prior hamstring pulls taught me the principles of RICE. The acronym stands for rest, ice, compression and elevation. RICE always helps the healing process. Because of RICE, I also ate a lot of Chinese food.

With this injury, it's difficult to sit or even lie down. The slightest touch to the underside of your leg i.e. chair, bed, causes your already tender hamstring further pain. The only time you get relief is sitting on a toilet. However, talking with friends or relatives in this position was easier said than done. The throne was quite comfortable, but no one wanted to have regal conversations with me.

So while my friends were gallivanting in beautiful Florida – walking, biking, and playing tennis, I went indoors and began physical therapy. Besides the painful stretching, I did a lot of kvetching. This way I thought, my therapist wouldn't push me as hard. My ears opened wider when he warned, "You wouldn't believe how many patients re-injure their hamstrings stretching.'"

Basketball and hockey players almost never have hamstring injuries. This is due to the strengthening of their "hammies" by running and skating backwards. Ballet dancers also don't have problems with these muscles. After physical therapy, I'll be in the pool "aqua jogging." This will be followed by running backwards and doing some "ballet *pliés.*" Therefore, when my Alzheimer's eventually kicks in, everyone will be familiar with my weird antics.

Now I'll participate in lower physical impact activities such as the photography club, trying to preserve my precarious sanity. I'll submit the print of my black and blue hematoma (Abstract category) in the annual photo contest. This photograph will also remind me to continue physical therapy and not get back on the tennis courts too soon.

Hamstrung is also a metaphor for being at an unfair disadvantage against your competitors. As you can tell, I'm hamstrung, bored and have mobility issues by this temporary setback, but it did give me time to write.

GOD'S GIFT

Achoo – **God** bless you!" is a common response to a person who has sneezed. Every time I hear the name God's Gift Achiuwa, a St. John's Univ. basketball player, I think it's God's blessing to that school. God's Gift Achiuwa is his authentic name. Perhaps, God's Gift (which God?)…the athlete gave to this Queens college, the prized talents of his basketball skills.

I saw God's Gift's first college basketball game at St. John's. God's Gift Achiuwa is a 6' 9" - 240 lb. His name is not a translation, nor changed in a court. His English speaking parents named him at birth in Nigeria, twenty years ago. "My parents told me I was a gift from God to them," he reveals. What a potential field day, New York's media will have with his name!

God is good; God is very, very good. His nickname though is "Gift" and with his physique, muscle, and athleticism, nobody's going to mess with what he wants to be called - at least not in front of him! As they say, he can be called anything he wants. I absolutely love playing with words, and with that name by God, it's a slam dunk. On the other hand, I probably should've used a pseudonym, writing these whimsical thoughts, Goddammit.

Strangely, God's Gift and I have some things in common, I'd like to share. (I'm sure you're wondering where the author is going with this. I'm smiling myself, as I can't wait to begin.)

In our primes, we are/were gym rats and basketball freaks. We both just about slept with a basketball. Being the only son, my mother at times, treated me as if I was a gift from God. (However, she was manic-depressive and most of the time yelled.) Living in her manic mood, which wasn't often, she'd called me "Ron Darling." Whenever she did, I thought I pitched for the NY Mets. Both Gift and I have siblings with religious names. Achiuwa is a very devout Christian, which influenced his enrollment at St. John's. Unbelievably and possibly with God's intervention, I bought a Catholic church, I really did. We're both in awe of the God-like Hall of Fame St. John's basketball coach Lou Carnesecca. Additionally, I played guard – (incidentally my wife also played – guard) when I competed in high school basketball. However, it's not all black and white, as we do have a number of colorful distinctions.

About a decade ago and across many ponds, let's go to Nigeria, where Gift was just another talented soccer player, participating in their national sport. His coaches recommended he give basketball a try, because of his gigantic height. At fourteen years of age, he was discovered by fellow countryman Alex Nwora, who's the basketball coach of a community college in Buffalo. Nwora periodically returned to his homeland to give basketball clinics. That's how Gift journeyed to Buffalo. Gift is a natural athlete with outstanding speed. He has a nice touch and quickly picked up the game. Gift is a good shot blocker, strong rebounder and superb on defense. God is truly everywhere! God's Gift was a third team junior college All-American before he transferred to St. John's. Similarly, I also went to college in Buffalo, so help me God. Incidentally, my oldest son (God's Gift has no son as yet.

Yes, I did think about bringing Jesus into the article) studied law at St. John's.

Gift's father, Mr. Achiuwa (*Gesundheit*) is a minister who with his wife raised six children. God's Gift's parents called their daughters Grace and Peace. They named their other sons, Promise, Precious and God's Will. Incongruously, I helped name my sister Faith. I wonder subconsciously, if something is not quite kosher in the Achiuwa house. Do God's Gift parents have doubts about the concept of one God? Blasphemously, they had two Gods (God's Gift and God's Will) living under one roof? - God Forbid!

God's Gift is intelligent, devoted and applies himself well in the classroom. In his first two semesters, his GPA's were 3.8 and 4.0. He's also a student of basketball and dreams of playing in the NBA. Gift has the perfect body, but is still learning the nuances of the sport. He's physically dominant and ambidextrous. Even though he hasn't developed his outside game, which would take him to the next level, he has tremendous upside potential. He states optimistically, "With the coaching I receive at St. John's, I'm hoping the path will be paved." From God Gift's lips to God's ears!

The journalists of the N.Y. Post, Daily News, and Times are praying that someday we'll hear, "God's Gift takes the floor for the New York Knicks at Madison Square Garden." Sportswriters' gift of punning, by God, will surely be tested. I sure hope to God, God's Gift turns out!

THE SAL TONES

I *definitely feel* like I'm on drugs!" Certainly, I had attained a "runner's high," pushing my body to the limit, while getting into the music from my iPod. Fellow neighbor and senior citizen Sal Mazzola and I were the only people working out at our Hamlet gym. Bantering, I told Sal the merits of using an iPod, since he wasn't listening to music. I buzzed, "Battling the machines with an iPod, lets you escape. You don't dwell on the repetitive sets or the clock. It allows your mind to wander."

A "runner's high" is associated with endorphins, a group of hormones occurring naturally in the brain, that when freed, give us the feeling of happiness. It has been shown; these biochemicals are also released enjoying music.

Recovering between exercise routines, I like to sit at one of the stations, catch my breath, and listen to my music. I enjoy it so much, I absurdly tell people, "This fitness center is really my *salle de musique.*" Incidentally, Sal's wife is a superb pianist with a musical "ear" who performs at the Hamlet. Being relaxed, I rambled to Sal, "Throughout my life, I too, have been called Sal." He smiled warmly as I related, "Friends thought my name Salmonson, was really two names, Sal and Monson. I'd tell everyone I was a cousin of the Yankee great Thurman Munson!"

By chance as I blathered away, the janitor of our community entered the facility. Believe it or not, his name is also Sal. It immediately hit me, we were three Sals. With music on my mind and still euphoric, I segued to the concept, "The three of us could form a singing group called the Sal Tones." Since no one was around, I put my arms around the two of them, pretending we were preparing to sing.

The hysterical part was the trio knew we couldn't sing at all! (Deep down every person would love to be able to sing well.) The custodian Sal, you see, wears two hearing aids, which severely limits his singing ability. He said, "I don't give a shit how bad we sound because I can't hear anyway." That cracked me up! Sal, my neighbor, rasped, "I can't sing either. My voice is failing. I've been bouncing from doctor to doctor, trying to find out what's wrong." I chimed in, "Both of you guys believe me, can still sing better than me!"

My speech communication skills are sorely lacking. I'm often impossible to decipher because I speak low and mumble all the time. I usually have to repeat everything I say. People always have that dazed look when I talk, which tells me, "Say it again." As a kid, I thought my name was "What." Whenever I spoke to my father, (who had a hearing problem) he would say, "What?" I really thought that was my name! However, there's one benefit from my mumbling I could positively cash in on. In semi-retirement I could easily get a part time job selling hearing aids. With my murmuring, I could make a fortune for the hearing aid company testing their patients!

Trying to sing, the three Sals exploded in uncontrollable laughter. As an aside, raucous laughter also releases these same hormones. Therefore that morning, I pulled off a trifecta of three activities that freed my endorphins; running, music, and laughter. Boy was I euphoric! (Maybe I should go back to the gym.)

What a great concept - make the gym into an endorphin center! I went home and searched the internet for other benefits of this chemical release. The list included - lowering blood pressure, reducing anxiety, slowing the aging process and helping depression. Surprisingly, other activities that give you that "rush" include crying, eating chocolate and having sex.

Since it's hard to incorporate eating chocolate, crying and having sex in our gym, we'll stick to the three basic concepts of aerobics, music and laughter to get this blissful feeling. By the way if you're interested in hearing us, come to the gym and bring an extra pair of underwear! Unsure though, if wetting your pants releases endorphins.

Don't shillyshally, the Sal Tones will be performing in the *Salle de Musique*, Tuesdays at 4 PM.

Ain't this silly?

Sal (sillysal@optonline.net)

TRIBES

Last week I attended the play "Tribes" which won an "Obie" for this year's best off-Broadway drama. This production portrays the dynamic relationships of a highly verbal, distressed, Bohemian family, whose parents are college professors. The members however, are seemingly deaf to one another. Oddly, the youngest member Billy in his early twenties, was born totally deaf, while the other family members have normal hearing.

Immediately and I believe with full intent, the audience has difficulty hearing the raucous, contentious, rapid fire intercourse in the play. The family has a thick British accent and the protagonist Billy has a garbled speech pattern, typical of someone born deaf. The play is also in the round and therefore periodically, the cast has their backs to you. The listener becomes conscious of Billy's oppressive solitude, as if he was living alone.

The audience soon learns the family has been unable to hear the needs of their handicapped son. Billy, who is quite intelligent, wears hearing aids and is an excellent lip reader. Unbelievably though, he has never been taught sign language, which frequently keeps him in the darkness of silence. The viewer picks up his inner pain and isolation. The audience literally experiences the hearing frustrations of Billy, as the show moves from one auditory intensity to another.

Billy meets Sylvia, his first love, who is starting to wear hearing aids. Her parents were born deaf and now she is slowly becoming deaf herself. She brings Billy out of the dark, while she's losing her grip on the hearing world. His girlfriend introduces him to the stirring passions of romance and the eye opening world of sign language. As I watched this particular love story unfold, the writer couldn't help wonder if ear foreplay was strictly off-limits. Would it dislodge their hearing aids or worse yet, trigger an electric shock?

More people suffer from some type of hearing loss, than any other serious ailment. Only twenty percent of these people seek help. When someone in a family has a hearing loss, the whole family has a problem. Audism is a word which describes the prevalent attitude and assumption that hearing people are superior to deaf people. Often the deaf are perceived as being dim-witted.

The audience almost feels as if they're eavesdropping, when they learn Billy's parents have chosen not to whole heartedly accommodate to his disability. His parents deliberately keep him away from the deaf community because "It insulates and isolates deaf people from the rest of the world." Later we hear the father's prejudice when he speaks of "The limitations of sign language, and the exclusionary cultures of the hearing and non-hearing." The question arises, "Is it not the inherent responsibility of parents to give their child every opportunity to succeed in this world; giving him all the tools he needs?" The child will decide eventually what he wants, when of age.

After studying sign language, Sylvia introduces him to the "deaf community." This group is about more than not being able to hear. It gives him membership in a strong, close-knit support group. Signing opens a new world, and this leads to a family cataclysm. Billy becomes transformed from a sweet son to a bitter person who refuses to talk to his family.

This passionate pitch perfect play strikes a chord on many daunting topics. Tribes is brilliantly acted theatre that makes you feel part of the action. It makes the audience open their eyes and ears to the many problems of the people of silence.

"The unspoken word is often louder than
any uttered words." (Anonymous)

Hear it while you can – Barrow St. Theater in lower Manhattan.

AUNTIE ANNA

My **Auntie Anna** was always the infamous center of our family circle. My mother was one of five children, all first generation Americans born of Polish and Russian descent. They were an extremely close knit unit, whose entire social network was family. They had few other friends. Her two brothers were both combative Type A personalities, who at the drop of a hat, were ready to literally fist fight. They also carried guns with them at all times. My mother was the youngest and Auntie Anna was the next to the oldest.

One Saturday night a month, they had a "family circle." They rotate their homes and only invite adults. Food of course, was always aplenty. Auntie Anna was by far the least bright of the brood. Invariably, she would say something outrageous (thinking back maybe she provoked them on purpose - nah) and the rest of the family would fiercely come down on her.

At every gathering the brothers would draw sides and one of them would come to her rescue. The intensity of these arguments would almost approach violence. If one brother made too much fun of her, there would be a reversal of roles, and the other brother came to her defense. This could even happen a few times a night. All of the siblings would get into these intense melees. The respective spouses sat there, listened but never really chimed in. It was as if they had front row seats at a monthly prize fight.

Days following the family circles, there would be post-game analyses of what transpired, via the new rotary telephones. My mother would call her older sister Tillie, then phone one of her brothers, and eventually Annie. Invariably my mother would abruptly end her telephone tirade with Annie, by slamming down the phone. The force was so vicious; pieces of the black phone would chip, exposing its white undercoat.

I always looked at my Uncle Murray (Annie's husband) and was absolutely shocked he didn't come to her defense. Uncle Murray was a clone of Rodney Dangerfield. He had the face, paunch, hair, voice, even cigar that easily made him a double of the comedian. My earliest recollections of Murray were when he worked in a fish store. At the age of three or four, I hated the smell of fish. I would vomit every time I was forced to go there. I think our senses were much more intense, when we were kids. He later became a cab driver who worked only at night. (more on that later)

In the 1940's, Anne and Murray moved to the Flatbush section of Brooklyn. They rented a one bedroom apartment in a six story building and lived on the first floor. In relatively quick succession they had three boys. The one bedroom apartment soon became ridiculously cramped. Auntie Anna slept on a couch her entire married life to free up a bed for her kids and husband.

Auntie Anna had a few quirks that made you scratch your head. She was a hoarder; saved newspapers, diapers, shoes, baby teeth, etc. Remember, they had absolutely no room. Fearful of robbers and not trusting anyone, she kept her coins in the oven. The paper money she also hid, who knows where? When my cousins were hungry, they'd heat the oven. (no microwaves) If they needed money for ice cream, they took change from the oven. Maybe the saying, "Money burning a hole in your pocket," evolved from her?

Uncle Murray never did well financially. After years at the fish store, he became a taxi driver. Annie never let him buy the medallion in order to own the cab, because she was embarrassed that he was a cab driver. Their neighborhood with time changed dramatically, as more lower class people moved in. In a few years, it was a dangerous place to live.

Their sons, all over six feet, survived the tight quarters, and incidentally all graduated college. In order for them to sleep in this one bedroom apartment, one family member worked all night. (they rotated) In addition, Murray drove his taxi only at night, for bed space. Their home was always quiet because at any hour of the day, someone slept. Slowly my cousins married and moved out.

To make up for the void of her missing sons, Annie adopted a dog she named King. There was no greater love affair than between Annie and her pet. King soon ruled the house. One particular jungle heat summer day Annie, the dog and Murray went for a walk. Murray was starting to fail medically from diabetes. Returning to the apartment, she immediately gave ice cold water to King. Murray sat obediently and waited for his drink, only after the King got his! When their grandsons visited, the dog wasn't accustomed to having young kids around. After King nipped her grandchild Ritchie, Annie's response was "What you do, to provoke the dog?"

Let's fast forward ten years. Ritchie (19) and his brother (17) were told to pick up Annie from the airport. The grandsons were devout followers of the "weed." (smoked pot) They only tolerated their grandmother when they were blitzed. Then they had a ball with her. As they left the airport, Annie was ticked off, complaining bitterly about them being ten minutes late. Ritchie, who was driving and looking for any excuse to smoke, closed the windows and lit up. The brothers passed the joint back and forth, with Annie in the backseat. Annie hadn't a clue what they were smoking. She got very upset though and asked, "Can't the two of you afford to buy your own cigarettes?" Fifteen minutes later, Grandma Annie made known, "For some reason I'm very, very hungry! The boys asked, "Do you want to stop at White Castle?" "Yeah, I've never eaten there," she replied. The three of them sauntered in, and as the result of the second hand smoke – Annie ate more than her two grandsons!

The neighborhood continued to deteriorate and my aunt and uncle became the only white people in the six story building. Then a catastrophe! – Uncle Murray died. This brought Annie much closer to her dog. She took him everywhere, even to bed. At a distant relative's wedding, as the bride watched in shock, Annie unashamedly filled plastic bags with roast beef, so afterward she could give the food to King.

My aunt lived a good number of years alone as the neighborhood continued to go downhill and fester with crime. At almost five feet tall, she was still cocky, feisty, and tough as nails. Annie now waddled like a swaying duck. In her nineties, (she safeguarded her age like no one else, even her kids didn't know) she let herself go. Her hair became startlingly carrot color, with a ring of snow white by her roots. (like a "creamsicle") She was unmistakable in many ways.

One Friday in August the temperature hit 100. That afternoon King died. Annie was shaken and broken beyond words. She phoned my mother and cried, "My King is dead, what should I do?" My mother, a little brighter than Annie said, "Call the ASPCA and ask for a truck to pick up the dog."

Annie phoned and received more bad news, "Our truck

has already made their rounds. You'll have to keep the dog til Monday." She recalled my mother and relayed the disastrous news. This time she bawled louder and more uncontrollably. My mother responded, "Call back and ask if you could bring the dog there before it closes." The spokesperson told Annie, "Sure, get here ASAP. We close at five." "I'll be there!" she said, and rang my mother to tell her the happy news.

Annie got a suitcase, stuffed the approximate sixty pound dog inside and headed out the door whimpering. (There were no suitcases with wheels then.) Annie incidentally weighed only about one hundred pounds. She was able to drag the heavy suitcase out the building, because she lived on the first floor. Once onto the street, she decided rather than get a taxi; she'd take the subway, only a short block away. (She was extremely frugal and thought there was enough time.)

It was Friday during rush hour, with stifling heat and the subway was packed. There were no seats. All the passengers looked at her, the suitcase, and wondered why she wept. At Franklin Ave. she got off, realizing there were no other white people. Now came the impossible part, she never thought about. She had to climb two flights of stairs to the street. She couldn't do it! She just couldn't physically do it! More and more people it seemed were looking at her crying.

A man out of nowhere came up to her and said, "Lady would you like a hand with that suitcase?" Her expression changed dramatically. She relaxed, even smiled and rejoiced, "You must have been sent straight from heaven!" She gladly gave him the suitcase.

The man took the suitcase, bounded up the stairs two steps at time, and disappeared into the crowd – never, ever to be seen or heard from again!!

P.S- Auntie Anna was the last survivor of her siblings. She protected her age so well as I said, that on her tombstone her sons literally picked a number – 94. At the cemetery, while shaking his head, her grandson Ritchie said, "She was out of her mind – but she wasn't stupid!"

TALKING ABOUT YOURSELF

I have a check-up appointment with my internist this week. While I think he's a good physician, I'm getting bummed, thinking he'll turn my office visit into a dissertation about his own health and life. This invariably elevates my blood pressure, which results in him increasing my hypertensive drugs. Routinely he'll ask, "How you doing? Are there any new medical problems?" After I tell him about my latest breakdowns, he'll reply, "I haven't had any of your problems, even though I'm older than you." As he takes my blood pressure, which is high, he'll add, "Mine is 120/75" exactly what I want to hear. He does give a great prostate exam; for that he gets big points. Maybe that's why I keep going there?

Is it just me or are my antennae on high alert, listening to people who only talk about themselves and have little interest in what you say? Yesterday, I told a joke which I thought was pretty decent. The acquaintance had that faraway look, dying to interrupt so he could spew out his joke, which of course he immediately told. Instead of listening to what's being said, he was already composing what he was going to say.

My mother would phone with the dutiful line, "How's the

family?" After my perfunctory answer, she'd explode into a diatribe of her problems, going on and on without end. It wasn't necessary to have a dialogue with her, just a few uhuhs intermittently. You could walk away from the phone, return with another uhuh, while you did whatever. This is so commonplace and flagrant that we've seen these comedic skits in numerous TV spoofs.

When I get these self-serving phone calls, I'll listen for a while and then contemplate how I'm going to get out of this. The best way - start talking and while you're talking, hang up on yourself! They'll assume there was a glitch because no one ever hangs up on themselves while they're talking. When the phone soon rings again, don't answer.

Talking about yourself is a widely found, egotistical tendency that can be used to your advantage. When applying for a job, I've instructed my sons, "Get the interviewer to talk about himself as much as possible." This could aid the evaluator hiring you, because everyone loves giving a dissertation about *numero uno*.

It's very easy to get turned off when a self -absorbed person focuses every conversation on himself. Don't they have a clue it's not a smart practice? This narcissistic individual thinks the world revolves around him; he's center stage and we're his audience. Their conversations are really monologues delivered in the presence of a witness. (Shouldn't there be a *witless protection* program? An organization devoted for these self-absorbed clueless people, from the consequences of their self-centered stupidity?) Don't they realized everyone eventually tries to avoid being in their presence? Selling themselves when they hold court often has the opposite effect; selling themselves short. After a while you get so aggravated, you give up trying to communicate.

Do people so wrapped up in themselves enjoy the sound of their voice or own stories that much? Usually, they totally disregard whatever non-verbal clues you give them; that you want out. If yawning, losing eye contact and turning away don't work, I desperately think, how am I going to get out of this? Typically, there's very little recourse and I'll be just plain rude, make up something, and walk away. The next time I see this person approach, I'll cross the street and pretend not to see them.

In all societies people who listen, learn more and usually have more success than those who talk a lot. Knowledge is attained by listening, as you never learn anything while your mouth is going. There's an American Indian proverb, "Your tongue makes you deaf." Every person has something to impart, and that's why I pay attention. A good listener also hears a great deal of what's not being said, i.e. body language, which regularly says a lot. By listening, you also earn the respect of the speaker. It's part of the definition of being a good friend. It has numerous benefits, including making the listener more popular.

I've seen self-obsessed "talkers" get hyped up, anticipating a new group of people. These newcomers' "virgin ears" will be bombarded with stories of the teller's self-importance. Some "conversation hoggers" only way of being entertained is to have people listen to them. They'll be your friend if you let them ramble on incessantly.

I wonder how they got to be so self-centered and insensitive. I never thought it was totally egotism, although big egos often have little ears. I've always felt they're insecure and uncomfortable with themselves. As a rule, they also have problems with silence, and tend to be more motor mouthed. People living alone have a higher tendency to talk a lot, but that seems logical. It's not gender specific, although it's known women talk more than men.

Interestingly, a study by the National Academy of Sciences (May, 2012) found; talking about yourself online such as Facebook, provides endorphin like brain activity similar to having sex or when eating. This of course explains why there's so much social networking online. I like most people, still prefer to get these brain activities the old fashioned way.

My blood pressure, as I said is an issue, and now that I'm older, I'm also more "puffy." In an effort to control my hypertension, I will try harder to lose weight, which often reduces these numbers. In addition, I plan to change my long term physician, who as noted talks about himself nonstop. However, do you know a MD who gives a good prostate exam?

KINDERGARTEN TO SOCIAL SECURITY

On September 8, 1950 Gary Harrison was bawling and carrying on, like many five year olds on their first day of kindergarten. He was desperately holding on to his mother's (Fanny) legs as tightly as possible. I was a head taller than him and couldn't wait to start school. Fanny pleaded, "Go with Ronny, I'm sure you'll have lots of fun." Little did she know, this suggestion started a lifelong friendship. We resembled the comic strip "Mutt and Jeff," and were inseparable from that day on. Coincidentally, we lived across the street from one another on E.27th St. by Brooklyn College. Soon thereafter, I took him every day to school four blocks away. Even though we were best friends, we fought at times. In the doll house we both wanted to be the father and a major brawl broke out. Gary lost two baby teeth and the doll house lost a couple of walls. Needless to say with my size, I easily won and he became the son. After that incident every five year old girl in the class avoided us, so we focused on the only female left, our attractive teacher. By the end of kindergarten, I taught Gary the subtle art of looking up our teacher's skirt.

There were millions of kids in our neighborhood and the

passport to acceptance was sports and humor. We emulated the "big guys" and learned almost everything about life from them. All major sports and New York's street games i.e., punch ball, stoop ball and box ball were played. We were among the oldest kids in our grade and that helped us excel in athletics. We were in the same classes through second grade and did well in our ABC's. These factors contributed to our self-esteem. At this young age Gary fantasized, "We'd be friends for life, and hoped our future wives would be too."

Although we weren't religious in our predominately Jewish neighborhood, we started Hebrew school in the third grade and went three times a week. We hated it because it cut deeply into our after school ball playing. Nevertheless, we quickly adapted and had fun. Eventually, we had a ball there, as our humor flourished. I had the ability to crack a joke with a straight face and get Gary in trouble constantly. The teachers wanted to know what was so funny and punish the offender. Gary, who never told on me, led the league in visits to the rabbi. New games such as Johnny on the Pony and Ringolevio were discovered. In time we even went early to play. Jewish friends from other schools heard about our fun and tried to transfer.

Gary and I would rush home from public school, change clothes and fly out to play ball. Periodically, I would forget my keys. All NYC apartment buildings have fire escapes and if you knew your neighbors in the same line as your apartment, (example 4J, 5J, and 6J) you'd ask them to use the fire escape. I lived on the sixth floor (6J) and knew my (4J) neighbors well. I'd climb out 4J's window and go up to my apartment. One afternoon, I told Gary, I didn't take my keys. Gary's building was across the street and faced mine. He lived on the second floor and loved to watch me climb the fire escape. He knew it was unbelievably scary. As you ascend, there's open space between every fire escape step. Gary played trumpet and as I climbed, he trumpeted out his window "Taps."

The entire neighborhood stopped to listen and then watched me climb up! His playing was hilarious because he played haltingly in a staccato fashion, cracking up between every note.

We were intrigued by our parents smoking, especially when they made smoke rings. We'd observe these delicate rings waft and float into the air. The tricks they did with the smoke rings were breathtaking! (pun intended) In the fourth grade we started our smoking careers. We'd steal cigarettes and hide them in bushes. At this age, "Salem" was our preferred mentholated brand. My father smoked Marlboros, but they were for "rugged men." No one really liked cigarettes, but they were better than the disgusting cigars we also tried. My mother never understood why I became so hooked on breath mints at this early age.

In the fifth grade, we learned the NYC subway, which opened exciting new journeys. Initially, we went to see our beloved Brooklyn Dodgers at Ebbets' Field. We lived and died with each game. To this day Gary and I know everything about our super heroes. Jackie Robinson's integration into baseball was talked about forever. Vin Scully, Dodger Hall of Fame announcer gave in addition to his superb play by play, philosophy of life.

By subway one Easter/Passover day we went to the zoo in Prospect Park. Our new friend Kramer (now the three musketeers) joined us. It was snowing and preposterously we brought "*Matzo*" sandwiches. The "lions" building was our favorite and ironically "The Lions Sleep Tonight was the #1 song at the time. The lions were sleeping when we arrived, but we decided to "rile them up." With no one around we threw Matzos into their cages to get their undivided attention. The three of us began to rumble softly but soon built it up to a full roar. This started a lion chain reaction (I'm not lying) that quickly became thunderous! Their ear-splitting reverberations echoed and caromed off the walls. When visitors walked in, they were scared stiff, did a complete 180, and high-tailed it out. (One of the three musketeers swears we also boosted their roars by introducing these African creatures to their first snowballs?)

Sleeping in each other's apartments was a natural extension of being best friends. After numerous sleepovers, we lulled our parents into these overnight arrangements. One day we each told our parents, we're sleeping at the other's house. Now Gary and I were free to do anything. By ten PM our normal bedtime we were tired, so we walked a mile to Kramer's private home. We snuck into his garage and slept, unbeknownst to him or his family. From these pretend sleepovers, we graduated to riding the subways into Manhattan and spending the night. We carefully avoided the cops and never feared the criminal element. We were young and just too stupid. Of course we couldn't wait to get home the next day - and sleep all day. Our parents thought we just had too little sleep and too much fun. And boy did we ever!

Humor was king in our neighborhood. Amongst our friends, no one ever said a sentence without some comedy being interjected. Naturally, everyone tried to top the other with their wit. Every form of comedy had its individual stars i.e. foreign accents, physical comedy, puns, etc. - Wry and dry humor flourished. (To this day I have trouble with the subtle differences between the two.) Absurdity always stood out; the more ridiculous, the more we loved it. Subtle comedy has always been my favorite; the kind that leads you down the path but lets the listener complete the humor.

In winter throwing snowballs at Brooklyn College coeds was a given. We also loved going "Up on the Roof" (first time I got high) to launch snowball rockets. We never aimed at anyone, but shook up a lot of people. Stupidly one day I was showing off and played the two snowball trick on "Yaver," a feared sixteen year old "hood." Everyone was scared of him because he'd beat the shit out of you, just for fun. I lobbed one high in the air; I saw Yaver observing its flight. While he watched the first one, I threw a second high speed snowball that caught him squarely on his chin. We took off, but Yaver knew it was me. Wearing galoshes I spun rubber as I fled. I attempted to jump a "cyclone" fence but slipped and got my neck impaled on the top prongs. As I tried to extricate myself, Yaver arrived and pummeled me mercilessly! From past experiences of getting hurt, I knew I couldn't go home and deal with my neurotic mother. The first thing she'd scream after I got injured was, "What did I do to deserve this?" Instead, Gary took me to his mother Fanny, who played Florence Nightingale. With my fingers, I stuffed the "kitshkes" back into my neck and she bandaged me. Nevertheless, when I got home my mother hit me anyway; for embarrassing her and not letting her nurse me. I was always indebted to my surrogate mother Fanny who tried to protect me from my own mother. She also kept me from getting stitches, while she often kept me in stitches.

Gary amazingly learned to ride his 26" two wheel bicycle in his apartment. Gary's father was in the linoleum business and his entire apartment had this flooring. These episodes could have been on U-Tube. (Internet wasn't invented) Gary broke furniture, banged into the walls, and yelled back at complaining neighbors. This was nothing compared to Fanny's shrieking. Gary was secretly proud of the permanent scars he created all over his home.

In high school we made the basketball team. The manager of our team lived in my building and stole the janitor's keys to the school. At night for pranks, a half dozen athletes (including Gary) raided the school for adventure. To this day I can still hear my heart exploding in my chest, as we stealthily explored in pitch darkness. Invariably, we'd end up in the unlit gym and play basketball. Depending upon the night and family obligations, there were a rotating number of friends in these capers. During subsequent break-ins, we decided to take things – sneakers, socks, jocks. One evening, (Gary wasn't with us) five athletes were caught by the police serendipitously. The incident made every NYC paper including the Times. All were thrown out of Midwood and finished high school at five distant schools. Gary was forever indebted to me, because I never ratted on him.

We both attended the Univ. of Buffalo and were in the same fraternity AEII. We weren't as close, because I skipped a grade in junior high and was a year ahead. He hung with a group of younger fraternity brothers who like President Clinton experimented with grass. (not sure if either ones inhaled) At the time I didn't know about marijuana and had fallen head over heels in love with my future wife. (If I smoked, I probably would've never gotten into grad school; I love to party.)

We've remained friends through all these years with only one interruption. I stayed in Buffalo for dental school and spent two years during Vietnam in the Army. My wife and I chose retirement in Florida so we'd be in close proximity to the Harrisons. Our wives are quite close, so Gary's prophecy of us all being friends came to fruition.

Every five years we celebrate our significant birthdays by vacationing together. For our 65th, we had a fabulous time in New Orleans with our third grade friend Kramer (third musketeer) and his wife. The six of us have been doing this since our fortieth birthdays.

"My father always used to say that when you die, if you've got five real friends, then you've had a great life."

Lee Iacoca

A ROCKY IMPRESSION

While in dental school, my wife and I rented an apartment above an Italian couple, who were in their nineties in Buffalo, NY. They had been married over sixty-five years and immediately adopted us. Every Sunday, Mrs. Luccio brought us platters of homemade Italian food. The aromas emanating from her kitchen made us weak with anticipation, weekly. Mr. Luccio was a retired barber, who had no hair. (Yogi Berra said, "Never go to a bald barber - they have no respect for hair.") Mr. Luccio had only four long front teeth that drifted all over the place. You wanted to look the other way when he smiled, which he did often.

Knowing I was a dental student, Mr. Luccio shyly asked, "Could you make a me some falsa teeth? I donta lika da way I look." "Of course I'll be glad to make you teeth," I enthusiastically countered. Needless to say, I neglected to tell him I never made dentures on a live patient, but presented a false bravado to instill confidence in my so called expertise. Moments later he told me he was a wicked gagger and feared X-rays and impressions because of this.

The initial exam entailed taking X-rays. Shockingly, he gagged so badly, my professors recommended "Novocain," trying to diminish his gag reflex. Mr. Luccio struggled and struggled attempting to make me look good in front of my professors. This upsetting experience should have been a forewarning. The treatment plan was to extract his four teeth, which would be easy, and make upper and lower dentures.

The dentures' clinic was a large thirty chair open room in which seven instructors carefully supervised. Therefore, almost a hundred people were in the clinic, including students and dental assistants. In the 1960's we were required to use Plaster of Paris for final impressions, in fabricating false teeth. It was mixed to a watery consistency, so the material would flow and pick up the details of the mouth.

We had practiced for hours of course on manikins to gain competency, before taking impressions on humans. I pretended to have the appropriate demeanor that I knew what I was doing. Mr. Luccio watched me carefully, as I mixed the powder and water, preparing this soupy Plaster of Paris. As I was nervous, he saw quite a bit of this material spill over the bowl onto my shoes. I then grossly over filled the impression tray to ensure I captured every minute detail. Watching this started him gagging a few times, in anticipation of what would ensue. Meanwhile, some of the thirty students had already inserted the plaster into their patients' mouths. Five or six of their patients already started to gag. This triggered a tidal wave of gagging in the expectant patients, readying for their impressions.

Mr. Luccio opened and I inserted this vastly overloaded soupy impression tray. As quite a bit of this material was swallowed, I envisioned the Plaster of Paris forming rocks and boulders in his stomach. I knew for sure – he was going to die! I pretended I had everything under control, and tried to act cool as a cucumber. Mr. Luccio started to bellow, as loud and as long as any fog horn you've ever heard! It was constant and then, the retching picked up in crescendo and volume. Everyone turned to see what was happening. The amount of perspiration dripping down my forehead was beyond belief. I was trying to keep the plaster in his mouth. (Keep in my mind, the patient and I knew if this impression wasn't perfect we'd have to retake it!) At this point I couldn't retrieve the boulders of plaster anyway that had formed in his stomach.

Four or five professors immediately sprinted over and gauged the dilemma. Mr. Luccio now was throwing up with the material/ tray still in his mouth. It was going all over the place. (This was before dentists wore gloves and masks.) The instructors also tried to wait until the material hardened. After it set they tried to take it out, as the ninety year old thrashed about in total agony. It was like grasping a moving target. They couldn't get it out; it locked in his mouth! The instructors now chipped the plaster away. The bellowing got louder and louder and I knew for sure he was going to die! I then thought I heard sirens from an ambulance, coming to pump his stomach or take him to the morgue; it was just my imagination. Finally, finally they got it out. I now had perspiration rings under each arm pit so huge they joined each other.

After ten minutes or so things calmed down, no ambulances, etc. and Mr. Luccio had regained his composure – I had not. He saw my perspiration and felt badly because he thought among other things; I'd be getting a failing grade. He took out his handkerchief, cleaned himself a bit and said in a fatherly broken English/Italian accent, "Don't worry. I'm a poor man, but I'll do as many haircuts as I have to - to pay back the cost of the material I swallowed!"

Follow up – The impression was successful or at least they didn't want me to take another. The denture made this ninety year old look like he had teeth of a twenty-five year old. (The patient helps in tooth selection and they all want to look young.) We had a nice laugh, when I told him the Plaster of Paris costs pennies. He wore the dentures a few times, only on special occasions. Every time he put the plates in, he gagged like crazy. My oldest son was born soon thereafter and the Luccios doted on him as if he was their own. I have this great picture of our new baby with Mr. Luccio, (without his teeth) and to this day I am not sure who had the sweeter smile.

JEWISH COWBOY

My Buffalo college roommate for three years Barry Cohen, recently married his psychiatrist. I would have paid a lot of money to have been a fly on the wall listening to their conversations. It was his second marriage. His first wife Micki, died of breast cancer. Micki, had her PhD in psychology and Barry has his in philosophy, but his strength also was in psychology.

Barry and I met in freshman year on the basketball court. We had both captained our respective Brooklyn high school teams. Barry was tall, strong as an ox, confident and totally fearless. After our workout, we had lunch at the university's cafeteria. While waiting on line with trays in hand, two humongous football players barged ahead of us. Barry who took no crap from anyone asked these oversized athletes, "What do you think you're doing?" I saw not only my college days, but my entire life being over, as he confronted these close to 300lb behemoths. After an intense face off, the two Goliaths meekly retreated behind us, and waited their proper turn. I was in awe of this Jewish cowboy.

We were shoo- ins for any fraternity we rushed, because we were jocks. At these rush parties with limitless beer, we had our first experiences with phenomenal live rock bands and dancing co-eds. These blasts were enhanced by alcohol and our raging hormones. At one party, they ran out of paper cups for beer. Barry took off his shoe, filled it with a large beer (size 13) and downed it. As senior fraternity brothers "rushed" him (after a few more size 13's), they craved this shoo-in. Thirty freshmen pledged AEII and elected Cohen their class president. Barry, a physically intimidating person, often had this bizarre, scowled, crazy look about him. With his strength and fearless persona, the older fraternity brothers were actually scared shit of him.

Barry was "off-the-wall." As mentioned, we played a lot of ball together. One time when Barry was in left field and I was in center, a ball was hit over our heads. I screamed, "Off-the wall Barry, off the wall!" Amusingly, I gave him that nickname which stuck. At times Barry was so wacky and unconventional he acted like a mental patient; bouncing off walls. Another description of him would be "offbeat." Ironically and playing with double entendre, he couldn't keep a beat; the worst dancer you ever saw.

In undergraduate school, Cohen majored in math but rarely studied. He said, "You either know it or don't, and they're no term papers." He spent the least amount of time hitting the books than anyone. The bulk of his nights, he played poker with major league card players in downtown Buffalo. He made a fortune, using his ability to memorize cards and know probabilities.

One blinding snowstorm during a Buffalo rush hour, Barry drove while I rode shotgun. We were headed into a heavily trafficked intersection in blizzard conditions. The roads were completely covered with ice and snow. Barry was driving very slowly but realized he couldn't stop his car! With oncoming traffic, he opened his door and jumped out. I couldn't believe what was happening and froze in disbelief. Incredibly, his swerving car with me in it did a 360, but somehow I made it across unscathed.

Returning to beat the university's 2AM curfew, Barry often

drove on sidewalks. There were always massive traffic jams because everyone was trying to beat the deadline. A cop stopped him and asked, "Why are you driving on the sidewalk?" He straightforwardly stated, "It's faster, there are no stop signs."

Buffalo in Erie county, had a well-known eerie mental institution. It could've been a perfect Hollywood backdrop for any horror movie. Fittingly, since my roommates were all pranksters, we pretended escaping from this mental institution. With Barry driving, me sitting shotgun, our third roommate sat in the back of Barry's two door sedan. We picked up a hitchhiking underclassman and motioned him to get in the back. With the three of us speaking gibberish, (we could've gotten an Academy award) Barry literally drove circles around a Buffalo city bus at 2 AM. Barry followed this up, by taking him on the wildest of joy rides. You couldn't imagine the petrified look on this young hitch hiker!

Cohen was the only person ever elected president of our hundred member fraternity for three years. When he spoke, he was as articulate and compelling as Demosthenes. As a mediator, he had the uncanny knack of defusing fraternal disputes.

In graduate school, now majoring in philosophy, Cohen attended a Black Panther rally during the height of radical racial unrest in the late 60's. The university's four hundred seat lecture hall overflowed with militants. Barry and a coed named Micki were practically the only white people in attendance. Barry got to his feet and gave a spellbinding "white person's response" to the chaos. Micki, working on her PhD in psychology, immediately fell in love with this articulate maverick. After a short turbulent engagement they married.

Ironically, Barry (Ph.D. in philosophy) and Micki raised two sons in a mansion contiguous with Thoreau's Walden Pond. Dr. Cohen became wealthy by working as a high powered consultant for a number of Wall Street companies. When asked exactly what he did, Barry with a glint in his eye revealed, "I'm a corporate shrink!" He made firms profitable by downsizing them. (Not the typical shrink) Extraordinarily, he personally spoke to every person he fired. He had the ability to do it so well, that after he let them go, they thanked him for the dismissals. He generated hope that these sacked employees could now pursue their dreams.

Barry and Micki tried unsuccessfully to have a third child. Instead, they adopted a black infant girl and named her Rebecca Cohen. Shortly thereafter, Micki was diagnosed with breast cancer. Unfortunately, after a long arduous battle Micki succumbed. When she died, their sons had already finished college and were out of the house. The young daughter however, was only seven. It was quite difficult for Barry, even with a live- in Nanny. Barry sought bereavement counseling, which brought him in contact with the psychiatrist, he'd eventually marry. Knowing Barry, I'm not sure who helped who more.

Barry Cohen aka, "off-the-wall", is an ethical (also his doctorate field) Jewish Cowboy who battles for righteous causes. (As an aside, he's an atheist, but can't shake his name.) His intelligence, charm and humor allow him to manipulate most situations. This extremely clever, exceptional man gave me a special gift – himself.

It's only fitting; I'll end with a quote from an esteemed philosopher from the Walden Pond, Concord, Mass. area.

> "A chief event in life is the day in which we
> have encountered a mind that startled us."
>
> – Ralph Waldo Emerson

BASEBALL, PASSING AND GENERATIONS

My big cousin Martin, who gave me all his hand- me- downs, died last week. Martin took me to my first baseball game at Ebbets Field to see my beloved Brooklyn Dodgers. He was about fourteen and I was eight. For me, that day was better than heaven on earth. My parents worked and had absolutely no interest in sports. I'll always have fond memories of that magical day.

Entering the rotunda, seeing the vast expanse of perfectly manicured grass, smelling the freshly cut green playing field, caused me to stop in my tracks and view the ballpark in total wonder. I had never seen the resplendent colors before, because when I watched the Dodgers, it was always in black and white. (before the advent of color TV)

Two days ago, I went to see an exhibition baseball game with a group of retired friends. I couldn't help think about the game, my cousin, and the countless precious memories. Baseball not only pervaded my life, but has played a rich role in society.

Baseball even today, can take you back to your youth. It returns to simpler times with less worries, responsibilities, and more smiles. You weren't as aware of the inexorable march of time. Baseball can make one pause and call time out, as time seems to stand still while the game is played. Time is measured differently. There are no hours, minutes, or seconds. Time is measured in strikes, outs, and innings. In theory, this timeless of all sports can go on forever.

At any game the stands are usually packed; an amalgamation of ages, races and nationalities. Nearly all fans are rooting hard for their home team. The passion is palpable and you feel the spirit of the moment. No finer bonds are the ones that bring father and son, grandparent and grandchild, family and friends together. Often the older generation teaches the next the basics of the game. There are many levels of appreciation of the sport. The novice can enjoy the game equally as well as the long term fan. And yet, there's not necessarily a hierarchy of age that makes one generation more knowledgeable than the other.

Baseball like most subjects has its own language and its words have crept into the fabric of our society. Terms such as waiting on deck, pinch hitting, getting to first base, throwing some heat, a cup of coffee have worked their way into our vernacular.

Understanding baseball initiated my first real adult conversation, with my Uncle Jimmy. I recognized we were now on an equal level in this area. When we'd argue the merits of certain players or strategy, I realized at the age of eight, he was a complete idiot. I knew more about baseball than he did. I had come of age. I then reasoned if my Uncle was such a moron in this area, he must be an idiot in many other areas. This is called the "halo effect."

I now have the privilege of going to ball games with my grandson David who's also eight. He's as ardent a Mets' fan as I. I really enjoy giving him pointers in the nuances and subtleties of the game. Teaching him the complex art of keeping score and watching his passion grow mean so much to me. I've told him in the privacy of our minds many fans play every single baseball position, manage, and even broadcast, while watching the game. Making baseball decisions, strategizing and second guessing, lets us fantasize we're on the field. All this is part of the beauty of the game. Given my grandson and I share baseball, we have greater potential for communicating in other areas.

Playing and or watching baseball brings you into a microcosm of life. It can teach an infinite number of lifelong concepts. Sportsmanship, competition, cooperation, and camaraderie are often first learned here. The importance of practice to achieve a goal can also be grasped at an early age. Taking one for the team, never letting striking out get in your way are all themes that will serve you well, in dealing with whatever life throws you.

It's even fun learning the history of baseball. The original field's dimensions were formulated probably by Abner Doubleday (1850) in a precise manner. The distances around the infield haven't changed since the game was invented. These parameters allow little margin of error for a fielder to catch a ground ball and throw out the runner.

My grandson was fascinated to learn baseball is considered the hardest of all professional sports. Many great athletes, who have played multiple sports, verify this fact. Hitting a baseball at the professional level, takes unbelievable athletic skill. Many pitchers have been clocked at throwing over ninety miles per hour. The batter has little time (.4sec) to decide to swing. The density of the hardball and speed of the pitch make it extremely daunting, even life threatening, to stand in the batter's box. Hitting is timing and the pitcher's job is to upset that timing by varying the speed of the ball. The pitcher can make the ball curve, sink, and even knuckle.

I told my grandson David in one's life it's a mere moment when a player can be an all-star one day, and soon this same player may struggle in an old timer's game. I don't think he fully understood that concept as yet. Reading this at a later age, he'll definitely understand what his Pa was philosophizing about.

Now I am probably past the seventh inning stretch in my life. (Though, I'm hoping for extra innings) The die-hard baseball fan waits until the end of the game before leaving. My cousin Martin died hard. He fought a long losing battle against cancer for seven years. This is one of the legacies this New York City police officer left me. He would have loved to have known I paid tribute to him and will always love the lore of baseball.

SHUT YOUR MOUTH AND OPEN WIDE

One of the many things that appealed to me about dentistry, not often discussed, was having a captive audience. We presume our stories and anecdotes are entertaining and never boring. On the other hand, everyone gets trapped by someone telling a shaggy-dog story. (long drawn-out story that impresses the teller as amusing, but to the listener it's boring) When the drill is whirling, we're at the helm and can steer the conversation to almost any subject. Clearly, it's extremely difficult for the patient to talk.

The word doctor means among other things - learned teacher. Teacher is a favorite word in all cultures, coming in not far behind the word mother. We all are indebted to our educators. As a dentist I often feel like a teacher, because I can impart tidbits of knowledge in various topics.

Dental dialogues are invariably one sided and these monologues are delivered in front of one or two people. There are little or no true conversations. I have the honor of practicing dentistry, and with drill in hand, receive the patient's undivided attention.

Before starting, the dentist in the hopes of trying to relax the patient begins usually with small talk. Sometimes these light casual conversations can become overextended by talkative individuals. The dental appointment has a finite time period to be completed. Accordingly, you can't allow the patient to have control of time. The ideal patient is one who knows when to shut his mouth, before someone else suggests he do so. With chatty patients my oxymoron, "shut your mouth and open wide" is always on the tip of my tongue.

Since there are exclusions to every rule, periodically I listen particularly hard to exceptional individuals. Bernard Baruch said something like, "Most of the successful people I've known don't talk very much, but when they talk, I listen." When treating these patients, my ears open wide, hoping to pick up some gems.

"Novocain" is administered hopefully, when the patient has stopped talking. In forty-five years I've had two patients who actually talked non-stop, even while I gave the thirty second lower injection. Astonishingly, they both spoke relatively intelligibly. This put me on high alert that they'd talk throughout the procedure, and they did.

My technique to interrupt these oral ramblers is to start the dental drill, pretending I'm warming it up. Sometimes, I feel like a maestro tuning my instrument before a recital. Most people have been conditioned from prior dental experience, to know when to zip it. While the patient is getting numb, my assistant steps outside the treatment room to get needed materials. However, as soon as she hears the drill, similar to Pavlov's dogs' conditioned reflex, she'll promptly re-enter. Thankfully, just a handful won't stop talking, due to their personality or nervousness. I never ever tell them to stop talking! As the handpiece is spinning, I accompany the drilling overture with "open wide."

If the patient continues to talk during treatment, the results don't come close to my standards. You repeatedly pray for these blabbermouths to hold their tongues. (they rarely do) Biting my tongue, (I'd figuratively like to bite theirs) thoughts go through my mind, to try anything to get them to stop. Isn't it ironic, people who have nothing to say, often babble the most. Sometimes I wish I was trained in oral surgery so I could wire their mouths shut!

When patients are numb, they frequently have no idea how their teeth come together. Therefore before anesthesia, I say, "Open and close a few times." This allows me to study their pretreatment occlusion. These observations aid in later replicating their original bite. Paradoxically, I'm asking them to shut their mouths before opening.

Choosing a subject to ramble on comes from anything I fancy. The topic is usually pleasing and not controversial. Occasionally, it might be sermon-like, without any religious overtones. (though the patient might be praying during the appointment) My monologues usually take some amusing path, aided by nitrous oxide or laughing gas. This calms down and loosens up the patient. When the patient recognizes he's completely numb and is breathing easier, I also unwind and let my natural humor evolve. Now completely relaxed, some patients I think wonder, "Is there a possibility of second hand nitrous oxide, because everything seems so funny?" (in theory no because of scavenger systems) Restrained humor is my goal. The humor has to be measured because the patient can't be bobbing up and down, laughing hysterically.

In semi-retirement, I like "open and shut cases." I enjoy treatment plans that are simple, routine, and straightforward. The dental heroics are reserved for my son, who's been practicing dentistry fifteen years. He chomps at the bit for these challenges.

Performing quality dentistry, keeping patients amused, and managing time, encompasses many skills. The dental restorations you create are functional art forms. Dentistry is a self-portrait of the person who does the work.

Therefore before I shut my mouth, "Try to autograph your work with excellence." - Anonymous

FLOWERS

The first time I ever picked up and really looked at a flower was right after a softball smashed into my Adam's apple. My error at third base when I was eleven years old cost our team the championship in a Brooklyn elementary school tournament. After the victorious team raucously left the field, I stood paralyzed for what seemed like an eternity, staring at the ground. I then noticed this little tuft of grass and minute flower staring straight at me. This tiny flower or weed had grown through a crack in the blacktopped paved field. It looked so proud, defiant and haughty, pleased with its heroic growth in uplifting the tarmac. This anomaly caused the ball to take a bad bounce and made me feel dreadful. I bent down studied it for a while, and then decapitated it.

I was raised in a Brooklyn apartment building and rarely saw flowers. During the "dog days of summer," I went to a public day camp located at this same schoolyard. Every day before we went home, the counselors made us weed this tarred ball field. This was the only time I ever "gardened." It was the first time I was introduced to botany. I got to know a lot of them.

The second flower I looked closely at was a "Rose." Her name was Elaine Rose and she was my first real girlfriend in high school. With biological hormones raging, she did of course, have a serious thorn issue. That thorn was her father! I had to be very careful; he was a complete drunk. He didn't work much and snored on a couch in the middle of their small two bedroom apartment. His presence often interfered with my "rose tending." Although as long as he dozed – foreplay arose!

In my first year of college, my next love was a Jersey girl; named also Elaine Rose. (I kid you not) This budding romance didn't last very long. However, I always wonder if I met another Elaine Rose, would I fall in love again. Was it the girl, the name, or a rose like lady I fell for?

Going off on a tangent, Eleanor Roosevelt was very fond of them. Astonishingly, both her maiden and married names were Roosevelt, (means rose field in Dutch) which I'm sure influenced her love of roses. After cultivating various roses she even had one named after her. She was very flattered at first, but when she read its description in a rose catalogue, she wasn't pleased. It said, "No good in a bed, but fine up against a wall."

Ironically, in my junior year, my relationships with flowers continued. I rented an apartment at 50 Flower St. in Buffalo and met the love of my life, Iris. It was the most exciting time of my life. Our love blossomed and everything came up roses. I was enraptured by her unfair allotment of gifts. Like the iris, Iris' life bows from the weight of her many talents and beauty. I was totally love-struck by this inimitable flower – and no, no she is not bearded. They say to have a healthy love of flowers; you must experience all types, including the wild and exotic ones. Looking back maybe my flowery affairs, were part of my ultimate destiny of bonding with Iris.

Iris' mom Lily also loved flowers and had two sisters, not surprisingly named Flora and Violet. Irises, as we know, come in just about all the colors of the rainbow. In fact in Greek it literally means rainbow. Growing up, her mom appropriately planted irises outside her bedroom window. Irises are easy to grow, take very little work, proliferate and don't cost very much. All these attributes of the iris, do not necessarily correlate with my wife's attributes. (She'll be reading this.)

My Iris made me think about flowers in other ways. In addition to their beauty and subtleties, Iris divulged "Butterflies remind me of flying flowers, and flowers remind me of tethered butterflies." She's also fond of the quote, "You can complain because roses have thorns, or you can rejoice because thorns have roses." – Ziggy. Though I never use it, my secret favorite proverb is "Stop and smell the Roses."

In general as we age, the more we enjoy flowers. Some elderly believe by becoming knowledgeable of them, you preview or get a jump start of what heaven is like. However, the almost hundred year old comedian George Burns said, "At my age, flowers scare me!" Actually, that's diametrically opposite to the truth. Flowers have been shown to be calming, can decrease anxiety, and lower blood pressure.

Iris and I think the name you're given might influence your destiny. A person named after a flower, makes us think of positive qualities such as beauty, love or peacefulness. Parents who named their kids Wilt or Gay for example, might negatively impact on their child's life.

We had two daughters and naturally named them Daisy and Fern. We waited an exceptionally long time for our son, as we had difficulty conceiving. We named him Arty, since Artificial wasn't a feasible choice.

THE DIN AT DINNER

Saturday night, my wife Iris, another couple and I were absolutely famished. We were half way home from a wonderful weekend in Princeton, N.J. Our friends recommended an Italian restaurant in Brooklyn but warned, "The restaurant was noisy, and there'll probably be a long wait." As we entered, we heard the **NOISE!** We were so hungry though, we decided to stay. "A hungry stomach has no ears." – Turkish proverb.

With "Hunchback of Notre Dame" shoulders, everyone leaned into our table trying to hear. After repeating our sentences many times, everyone had that glazed look, pretending we heard one another. Noise became not only an intrusion, but also a disruption of thought! (Studies show loud sounds increase blood pressure and breathing rates.) Our hungry group became agitated and less sociable. I was desperate to eat, but the noise was eating at me.

The tables were packed so tightly, you heard your neighbors' attempts of conversation. The music was too loud and the eatery had no carpeting or curtains to dampen the sounds. Its' open kitchen and hardwood floors also increased the clamor. These dynamics caused an echo chamber of reverberations that ricocheted off the walls. In response, we ratcheted up our voices, speaking even louder. My friend Howard, who is preposterously, a sound engineer, had an app on his IPhone, which measured the noise level at 100 decibels. The most common word bellowed out at every table was "What?" But maybe, just maybe this raucous noise was done by design?

Subconsciously, the louder the noise the faster you eat so you can depart. Obviously, rapid table turnover is great for business. Brisk turnovers cause the cash registers to "ka-ching" more, which ironically translates into more dins. By gobbling down the food, your gastrointestinal reflex of being "full" doesn't kick in. It takes time for the meal to be digested and reach a "satiated" blood level. This feedback signifies you're satisfied, and causes you to stop eating. Hence, fast eaters devour more food. Of course these additional intakes translate into more profits.

Noisy restaurants in general, serve larger portions and have more obese patrons. Fairfield Univ. (1980's) showed chewing rates increase by 33% when music is in the high decibels. A study in France (2008) revealed men drank more alcohol at these levels. Consequentially, people eat and drink more, eat faster, and leave sooner because of the racket. Therefore, boisterous restaurants tend to be more profitable.

After poor service, Zagat reveals noise is the second most common complaint about restaurants. Is it time for Zagat to have noise ratings also? Yes, especially now that I'm past sixty-five and have some hearing loss. As an aside, individuals with hearing aids have more problems with noisy restaurants than normal hearing people. Hearing aids paradoxically, can't selectively filter out extraneous sounds and amplifies all sounds. I hunger for a restaurant where you can exchange quiet conversations in a serene setting. Quiet establishments tend to be more upscale with better food and service, but costs more dough. One must decide if it's worth the extra bread.

There are some benefits eating at these earsplitting

establishments. Besides being faster, which helps if you're in a rush, they're usually cheaper. When patronizing one, you can purposely not talk to your spouse, companion, etc. if desired. Parents can bring their screaming, spoiled brats and sometimes have them go unnoticed. Additionally, there are more doggie bags because you want to leave ASAP. You're also free to spill your inner most secrets, given that no one can hear you.

Shockingly, there were five teenagers eating nearby, who didn't talk. They were texting and didn't make a sound. I wondered, "Were they texting each other?" Maybe these devices will help save our hearing in the future? Going off on a tangent, there's even scuttlebutt of child-free restaurants evolving.

In these din filled restaurants, AARP advises members to sit in booths rather than tables. Look for carpeted areas and table cloths, which likewise help. Park yourself away from the kitchen and always sit in alcoves or side rooms, with your back against the wall. To further aid hearing, face people who are chatter boxers and sit beside mumblers. When ordering point to the menu or blackboard, so the waiter gets your choices right. Even better, ask the waiter if he's trained in lip reading!

Restaurant employees not casual diners suffer most from the daily dose of decibels. Besides workers chancing hearing loss, these loud dins have been correlated with cardiovascular problems. (Neitzel, R. Univ. of Michigan environmental noise expert)

To stem hearing loss, someday these restaurants might dispense ear protection devices, such as ear plugs or hats with ear flaps, although I doubt it.

"Keep Your Mouth Shut and Your Ears Wide Open" is an old English proverb. When eating in noisy restaurants maybe it should be the reverse!

As a follow-up, the waiter who I'm sure couldn't hear us, served two of the four dinners incorrectly. Anyway, we wolfed down the meal, took our doggie bags and flew out of there.

EXCESS BAGGAGE

I was neatly packing my almost ready for garbage clothing for our trip to Spain, celebrating our forty-fifth anniversary. I thought how difficult it is for me to throw clothes away. Growing up, I loved getting hand-me-downs, especially from my admired cousin Martin. However, as I was cramming my suitcase, I worried about it being overweight. It ticks me off paying excessive baggage fees.

Most people return from vacation with more than they took. It's a slam dunk for us. Buying clothes, souvenirs, or gifts for the grandkids is our norm. To make room for these purchases, I wear old clothes and throw them away, trying to stay below the baggage weight restrictions. Many travelers know this concept, but I have my Ph.D. in it. I bring old underwear, socks, sneakers, etc.; things that are falling apart. I really don't care what I look like, since I'll never see these people again. In contrast my wife doesn't buy this concept, and wants to look good all the time.

As an aside, I remember reading about an obese mother and daughter who were not allowed to fly Southwest Airlines unless the two, bought four seats. This is part of their "Customer of Size" or "too fat to fly policy," which most airlines have but rarely enforce. Four tickets were necessary because their size encroached upon the comfort of others. (Now these two transatlantic passengers could get four meals!) Wouldn't it carry greater weight, if airlines had a total maximum weight for each passenger and their baggage? Their new slogan might be - "Pay less by weighing and packing less." This could result in reducing "excess baggage."

On this trip my wife and I met an exceptionally compatible couple who were octogenarians. Surprisingly, they were very youthful and entertaining. After a few glasses of wine, I found myself one on one with this bright lady. I was stunned when she said, "We've been dating only nine months and both married before. However we live separately in Florida." I then asked, "What's your secret in choosing a companion?" She replied without hesitation, "Pick someone with the least excess baggage. In other words, select a mate with the least problems with their exes, kids, health, and money." More easily said than done I thought, but I knew she was right. I ended our exchange bantering, "I guess it's easier to hug and love, if there's less baggage to lug!"

My wife and I pigged out on Spain's delicious tapas. Voyaging for the first time in Spain was not the place to count calories!

However, my old clothes became ridiculously tight as I gained some pounds. At one restaurant I heard a Spanish waiter say what sounded like "*Vaca Gorda.*" I had no idea what it meant, but I it seemed related to food.

I really didn't really care that I couldn't close my soon to be discarded garments. However, I hadn't taken enough clothes and that bothered me. Consequently, I eyed a fellow vacationer, who was about two sizes larger than me, who was also eating splendidly. Knowing my dilemma, I had an epiphany which I told my wife, "I wonder if he'll also be throwing away his old clothes? Before I approach him, do you think I could get into that guy's pants?" I'll never forget the look on her face!

Learning more about art history was one of the highlights that climaxed at the Prado in Madrid. I was particularly impressed with the hefty collection of Ruben's paintings. Rubenesque applies to women he drew who were attractive, well fed and overweight. It was a sign of aristocratic opulence because these women didn't work much and their calories went effortlessly to fat. Ironically, my father was a Rubin (Rubin Salmonson) who chose a Rubenesque woman. (my mother) Regrettably, like members of her family, I've inherited her genes and carry extra baggage. Loads of my relatives seem to be digging their graves with forks and knives.

After vacationing, I visited various physicians, before wintering in Florida. Now that I'm on the wrong side of my seventh decade I see more doctors. With my newly acquired extra baggage (weight), I enter their offices with trepidation. In one office I joked, "I just got back from vacation with some surplus baggage, even though I shed some excess baggage." Since they didn't have a clue what I was talking about, I had to explain. A Spanish speaking nurse liked the line and snickered. At that moment I recalled the Spanish waiter's phrase and asked, "What does *Vaca Gorda* mean?" "Fat Cow" she replied. – I still wince.

One doctor went into his spiel of extra weight correlating with high blood pressure, heart disease, and diabetes. Of course, I am either on deck or have these problems already. My gene pool is poor; a more apt term might be my "cesspool of genes."

I promised my physician to diet and exercise. The first thing they say you lose when you diet is your sense of humor. I don't want to blow that. A diet by the way is the price you pay for going over the feed limit. Fortunately, I just heard a great new way of losing weight. You can eat anything you want, but you have to eat naked with other naked fat people!

Therefore, I'm now looking for dieters with excess baggage to join me. Any takers?

BARBERING - DENTISTRY

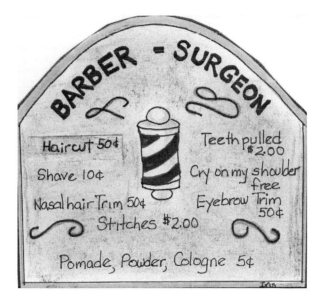

I tried a new bustling barber shop near my Florida retirement community. There were five or six chairs, all occupied with the exception of one. A number of patrons were waiting for their favorite barber. The barber not working tapped his chair and said "right here." Taking me off guard, I wasn't sure why this particular guy was available, with so many people waiting. The thickly bespectacled barber was surely an octogenarian, and totally bald. I thought of Yogi Berra's line, "Never go to a bald barber; he has no respect for hair." Always being in a rush, (being semi-retired I'm not, but it's drilled into me) I made the hairy decision and chose the empty chair. I felt sorry for him, but soon I thought I might be sorry for myself. As the saying goes, "the difference between a good and bad haircut – is two weeks

While in the chair, I reflected on the many similarities between my chosen profession of dentistry, and being a barber. Despite not paying attention in dental history, I learned in the Middle Ages barbers often did extractions. Today both professions use adjustable chairs and can work standing. Each brings sharp instruments to their patrons' heads and usually converse pleasantly. Both occupations command respect. You're entrusting these caretakers, not only to make you look and feel good, but to perform these procedures safely and gently. Their labors result in us being well groomed which boosts our self-esteem and self-confidence. Admiration frequently develops for these practitioners because of their talent and efforts.

First haircut/dental visit, often are part of our "rites of passage." These events sometimes even photographed, become etched in our memories. At these early events, parents should hammer home the importance of being a good patient. Everyone benefits from this mutual cooperation with the consumer consistently getting better results.

We've all seen incredible makeovers in people having their hair and/or teeth done. The results can revolutionize personalities. People who have bad hair or an ugly smile can be changed relatively quickly, into a Cinderella or Adonis. Recently, I transformed a fifty year old woman with huge spaces between her teeth. She actually cried when I gave her a mirror (both occupations utilize) and saw her new beautiful smile. Incidentally later she also cried, when she saw the bill. Everyone has marveled at a new coif, dramatically improving a person's appearance. As a dentist I've wondered, if a person had only one choice between getting their hair or teeth done, which esthetic makeover they'd select.

I've told barbers, "I can tell if a patient is a good dancer by how they respond, while I'm treating them." Similar to a woman following her dance lead, the patient will shift and turn, responding to my movements. The male patient doesn't react nearly as well because he's not accustomed to being led. Patients are shocked when I remark, "I know you're a good dancer." They think I actually saw them dance someplace. Barbers, who likewise position their customers, smirk and agree saying, "I never heard anyone say that." Frustratingly and sometimes amusingly, there are some spastic individuals, who react diametrically oppositely to anything you ask.

Since I'm now "folliculary challenged" I have less hair to cut. I therefore questioned, "Is the cost reduced for people with less hair because it takes less time?" In dentistry, patients with few teeth are charged less for cleanings. The barber replied, "Since there's less hair, I take more time, because it counts more." I really didn't follow this, but since he had sharp instruments, I thought it's best not to be contentious. In actuality, most barbers usually give senior discounts; it is faster to cut *"alta cockers"* hair. As an aside, my haircutter spends more time trimming my eyebrows, ears and nose than working on my dome. I guess he feels this justifies the full cost. Why do we lose hair in places we want to keep and grow it in undesired areas? I actually investigated the teleology. (study of purpose or design in nature) There were no valid reasons for this absurd hair growth. I ponder by looking so bizarre; does nature select you to be planted sooner?

This barber had many religious icons displayed around his chair. As he took off my bib I said, "In both professions we deal with bibical acts." He gave me this weird look which meant, no idea what I was talking about. I then replied, "I was playing with the word bib." It was still way over his head! Ironically, barbers and dentists are the only people whose conversations you can follow, even though it's over your head.

Now in semi-retirement, I'm thinking about reinventing the old barber/dentist work place. Appropriately, I'd like to begin my dual career working on barbers. I wonder when a dentist treats a barber, who does the talking? Since I'm semi-retired, I'll barber on men and women in my age bracket. Both populations have hair problems; with women it's tint and with men it ain't.

Since there are no combined textbooks in this dual field, common sense dictates, do the hair first especially if the same person needs an extraction. Extractions can get hairy, especially with complications of the aged. Since pulling teeth could be upsetting, I'll execute them out of sight in a private area. Come to think of it, my beginning haircuts definitely won't be "out of sight." However, the people on whom I practice my barbering - might want to be! By the way, that's where I was - after the haircut this new eighty year old barber gave me.

CONFLICTS IN BEING A SLOB

Nice Outfit" I sarcastically greeted my more than overweight psychiatrist, as I entered his office. He was wearing an enormously sloppy shirt that hung outside his pants, in a not too professional manner. I'd been thinking about changing my therapist for a while, as I've been on a bad roll and felt he wasn't helping enough.

Ironically, I've also been wrestling with this current dress modality. I have trouble wearing my shirts outside my pants. Tucking your shirt inside your pants had always been the standard. If my shirt was not tucked in, my mother would invariably say, "You look like a slob with your shirt out." Recently, a friend's thirty year old son professed, "Every guy looks like a dork, wearing his shirt inside his pants. Only guys over sixty years old wear them inside." Hence the conflict unfolds. No one wants to be called a nerd and of course, no one wants to go against his mother.

Everyone is taught being well groomed counts. Physical attractiveness is a universal criterion for predicting a person's success. "Looking Good" is a global axiom that is strived for in every country and culture.

"Looking good" is enhanced by watching your weight and dressing well. Wearing baggy clothes outside your pants hides your physique. In my opinion, this mode of dress makes an obese person look thinner and an average person heavier. I believe you should be rewarded for your efforts in caring for your body. The outside the pants dress is really counter to our "Nation's War on Obesity."

Talking to my therapist I segued into this baggy dress look. I stated, "On my maternal side, my mother, aunts and sisters were quite obese. They all wore Moo-Moo dresses." (A Moo-Moo dress is a large tent like outfit, with no waist, worn by women who become too large.) When I was young my friends and I, behind their backs mocked, "Moo-Moo dresses are worn by slobby women who resemble cows." My psychiatrist's ears perked up when I made known, "My mother" who was large herself, periodically threatened my sisters, "I'm sending you to Camp Fatopia." This was a sleep away diet camp, where you wouldn't worry about being ridiculed for your enormous size. Incidentally, my family members were not fatorexic. (thinking of themselves as being too thin, hence eating more - opposite of anorexia) I added, "I always disliked that large look and vowed I'd never to marry a woman who was obese." As an aside, my rather rotund psychiatrist squirmed in his chair as I blathered away.

Let's address some good points about wearing your shirt outside your pants. It saves time and money not having to buy and wear belts. You can also extend the life of your pants, because no one sees your partially opened trousers with their zippers and buttons straining. (No, this paper hasn't been subsidized by the National Belt, Pants, Button, and Zipper manufacturing lobbies.) In addition, it's harder to tell if you've gained weight. To boot, you won't miss that waist rollover inverted look whenever you've bulked up. We all know old pants never lie when it comes to telling us if we've gained. The shirt over a man's zipper might also help incontinence problems. How did this trend come about? Was it because there are so many overweight people who didn't want to buy new clothes? Did they expect to lose weight?

My psychiatrist obviously not comfortable with my diatribe on dress and obesity changed the topic. He asked, "How was your trip to Eastern Europe?" He was surprised when I told him, "While there, we booked a side trip to Slobania (I kid you not) in Romania. My mother's family came from there. I always thought Mom was never proud of her small, poor, underdeveloped ancestral area. Slobanians (Slobs) were also looked down upon by their neighbors."

I then had an epiphany, as I heard my mother's voice reverberating, "In the land of Slobs, we didn't want to be slobs." This most definitely influenced her dress code. Ironically, when we visited this antiquated place, every citizen wore their shirts inside their pants! We paid a visit to some distant relatives, with the same surname as my mother's maiden – Sobotkin. (I debated whether to convey this, as it might lead to identity thefts.) I remember my mother's brother, Uncle Phil always having a twinkle in his eye when he told people his last name – Sobotkin. Immediately he'd say, "Just shorten it and call me a S.O.B." In the land of the Slobs, they all were S.O.B.s. My mother incidentally sobbed more than all her four S.O.B. siblings. My therapist couldn't hide his grimace when I reflected, "I wanted to inscribe on my mother's tombstone; "Here lies Dotty a certified Slob, a S.O.B., who raised her kids never to be slobs."

Upon leaving I noticed my psychiatrist, shaking and shaking his head. I paused at the door, turned around and waved. I then knew I was in search of a new psychiatrist to help a "dress" my many issues.

For my wife – Iris

45TH WEDDING ANNIVERSARY

It's only fitting on our 45th wedding anniversary to reminisce. Ironically, we were both born in '45 and met in college at Buffalo. The top hits that year on 45's were "So Much in Love" by the Tymes and "You're The Best Thing That Ever Happened to Me" by Gladys Knight. I fell passionately in love and courted Iris for a long time. Looking back, it was the time in my life I felt most alive. I found the one I wanted to go through life with.

We celebrated this milestone by taking our family of ten on a Princess Cruise. It barely came about as our oldest son Scott, ruptured his Achilles tendon and was hobbled. One week before his wife Lisa, had unexpected hernia surgery. There were also ominous predictions of a major hurricane. (Irene) These land lubbers knew a smooth sailing might not be on the horizon.

Scott brought a wheel chair, crutches and scooter (more on that later) to navigate the ship and port excursions. These devices were a godsend in aiding his mobility and gave the group an unexpected free pass to the front of every line. (next trip consider the "wheel chair ploy"- rent one and someone feign injury)

Scott's wife Lisa pulled a faux pas when she answered "yes" to

131

the medical question – Do you have nausea or diarrhea? She was of course above board with her reply. But after hernia surgery, her meds caused these problems; technically she wasn't sick. The group had to wait for the ship's physician's approval before she could board. We were proud how Lisa handled her post-surgical healing. By the end of the trip, she was in ship-shape.

One week before the trip, I apprehensively discovered we were leaving from Brooklyn. Even though I was born and raised nearby, I never knew cruise ships disembarked from there. This uneasiness was soon dispelled as the port was closer to our homes, more accessible, and easier to park.

Our three cabins were located midship and on the same deck. Our quarters had interconnecting balconies adding to the festive atmosphere. The kids loved having bunk beds that pulled down from the ceiling. It made sleeping adventuresome. I taught the word "port" to the grandkids, as our rooms were located on the left side of the boat. Their grandmother was our only portsider and they were surprised when I shared, "Lefties were believed to be both more artsy and off the wall than righties."

With anchors aweigh and all hands on deck, we departed Brooklyn and captured the magnificent views of Manhattan, Statue of Liberty and the Verrazano. Many travelers immediately developed "index finger tendonitis" photographing these sites. Fortunately, this didn't slow them down when it came to eating.

Our family soon learned the ropes at the eating extravaganzas, or better named "gastronomical orgies." I knew we'd be bad, but never did I expect us to be so gluttonous! It reminded me of the Catskills, where waiters brought tons of food at every meal. If you couldn't wait to be served, you could pig out faster by running to the buffets! If you were even remotely hungry, they had 24/7 stations serving hamburgers, pizza, and ice cream. (The kids had ice cream two or three times daily.) Everyone gained weight;

it was a question of how much. My pants soon cried, "Mayday, Mayday," and finally couldn't close.

Our first port was Peggy's Cove in Halifax, Nova Scotia. We were enraptured by this throw back in time fishing village with its' famous lighthouse. Located on a treacherous rocky shore, this photographer's paradise is "one of the most snapped spots in Canada."

Sara (fourteen but looks much older) was hot to trot to see a hypnotist perform at the ship's vast theater. The hypnotist asked for volunteers who were over eighteen. Sara went ballistic, flailed her arms, and was chosen as one of the twenty participants. Following the hypnotist's suggestions, she closed her eyes, relaxed, and quickly fell into a trance. The participants who were seated closely, gradually slumped onto the shoulders of one other. Later Sara recalled, "I was conscious of my surroundings, but still couldn't wait to belly dance and milk the cows." The show was exceptional and a treat to watch our other spell bounded grandkids observe their older cousin.

As the days passed the family went on cruise control. Sara (14) and Lauren (10) hung out together as did David (9) and Jaime (7). Everyone enjoyed Rodrigo's (a steward) animal arrangements made from towels. In an effort to exercise, most took the stairs rather than elevators. Some utilized the gym's treadmills and that became interesting when hurricane Irene approached. You really had to hold on as the pitching and swaying made the machines precarious to use.

My sisters gave us an anniversary gift certificate to the ship's spa and beauty salon which we used on the kids. It was a treat to watch our granddaughters' excitement having their hair and nails done. At the entrance to the facility I had to sign in for them. I (Pa) signed "Frank Necrosis" and taught them its meaning. (direct, straightforward - decay) They were shocked and flabbergasted. I of course, loved it even more. Someday they'll realize Pa loves to play on words and is sometimes naughty. Maybe they'll even notice I used a bunch of "nauti – cal" terms throughout the article.

Every night and I mean every night, we took family photographs. There's always occasions in every family's timeline when you pose for one. It's a source of pride for parents and usually a dread for the kids. Everyone dresses in coordinated outfits and hopes these photos will be forever treasured. Nevertheless, when we think of loved ones no longer with us, we remember them from these treasured pictures. These portraits are usually most cherished by the generation that looks the best. The scuttlebutt; the middle generation typically looks the best and prizes them the most. The other generations don't care as much if this time is chronicled.

Next stops were the quaint picturesque town of Bar Harbor, Maine and scenic Acadia National Park. The state's granite mountains merge with the sea and offer one of the most spectacular settings on the east coast. Cadillac Mountain is the highest point in the North Atlantic and the panoramic views were breathtaking. (double entendre)

In Maine and the remaining ports, the adults had lobster for lunch and dinner. Maine lobster is considered the most delicious shellfish in the world. Out of six meals, we had lobster in some form - five times. The only mistake we made was not having it the sixth. Preposterously, the kids who can get away with it, ran for ice cream as soon as the boat moored.

In Boston we split up, the four girls shopped while my wife, Jaime and I walked the Freedom Trail with the guys. Scott used his knee scooter to negotiate historic Boston. A knee scooter is a four-wheeled alternative to crutches or walker, used as an ambulatory aid. You rest your injured leg on a cushion, and push with the other foot and glide. The maneuverability and speeds Scott attained were amazing. He was a real trooper who never complained about his handicap, despite having problems at times with the cobble stone streets.

Jaime (7) was absolutely fascinated learning about the American Revolution. She cried when we didn't have time to explore the "Boston Massacre" museum. Other tantrums did occur, some thrown by our grandson and some by me. One night, trying to avoid a conniption, I threw a few "down the hatch" but never really got "three sheets to the wind."

At sea we heard the distressing news of an earthquake whose epicenter was in Virginia. At the same time heading directly towards us, hurricane Irene brewed. In these unchartered waters we raced back to Brooklyn. There were fierce winds, torrential rains and huge whitecaps. (fortunately my younger son and I are dentists and we're used to dealing with "white caps") The crew battened down the hatches and our group became very anxious.

Outrunning hurricane Irene and safely back in harbor, we exited first (because of the wheel chair) and watched in wonderment as a porter packed our cars to the gills. (I'm sure he had his PhD in spatial relationships.) We dashed home striving to beat the storm so we could stow our outdoor furniture before Irene hit. (Scott on crutches couldn't help.) It was a harrowing but safe ending to a wonderful commemorative trip.

As I contemplate our forty-five years, I muse over my father-in-law Les who died at ninety-three. He had two attentive and devoted wives. Iris' beloved mother died after forty years of marriage. As a testimony to that matrimony, he married a wonderful woman, and that union lasted nineteen years. Both spouses were fantastic! (Yes, they couldn't do more for Les!) At his ninetieth birthday, with family assembled, he spoke of his "riches." (No, not in the monetary sense, though he was upper middle class) He tearfully and haltingly spoke of his great wealth in having a beloved family stating, "surpassed all material possessions." Then unbelievably he quoted Ben Franklin, "Those who love deeply never grow old, they may die of old age, but they die young."

Even though our wedding was many, many years ago, the celebration continues. In life it doesn't matter how much money you have, possessions you have or where you go.

It's who you have by your side.

CAVITY

The universal desire of every kid is to have a dog. My two sisters and I lived on the top floor of a six story apartment building in Brooklyn. We begged and begged our mother for a dog. She tried to hold back her smile as she said, "Why should I get a dog, when I have three already?" She laughed and laughed.

It seemed inevitable when I had my own family, we'd get a dog. Growing up my wife had a great experience with her beloved "Princie" a gorgeous boxer. My two sons (eight and six) were excitedly chomping at the bit. Our criteria for selection were; getting a pup, it being mid-size and one that didn't shed. I of course added, "I wanted one with a sense of humor."

Our family drove to a suburban kennel, and chose a pedigreed Airedale terrier, the cutest of the litter. We called him Cavity because I'm a dentist, and hoped this whimsical name might shape his personality.

When he was a pup, I'd lie on the floor, get real close and watch him drink his water. I'd do this often and decided it would be fun, pretending to drink his water. Eventually, he hated it and growled. That's how I taught him his first "trick" whenever I gave him water.

Soon we noticed our totally hyper dog was different from all other dogs. The dog was nuts! He seemed allergic to people, as he barked and howled furiously. He only wanted to be around other dogs. He broke the record for the most number of times running away. My wife was the only person he barely tolerated. He acted as if he was "king" of our family, and we were his personal attendees. We decided to take him to obedience school, which he failed miserably. Whenever we brought him to a kennel, he couldn't care less if we ever picked him up.

I asked Jerry our veterinarian and very close friend, about Cavity being mentally retarded. "In any animal species there must be a bell shaped curve of normal behavior "I reasoned. Jerry agreed with the normal curve concept, but since he knew me, thought our problem was probably a mismatch between the dog and yours truly. One Saturday night, after a date with the vet and his wife, we returned to our house for coffee, cake and a "behavioral test." Cavity didn't like being wakened from his deep sleep and broke the dog high jumping record, when greeted by this stranger. He growled ferociously and tried to leap out a closed window in his flailing attempt to escape.

After a few other tests Jerry said unequivocally, "This dog must be put to sleep. Soon, he's going to bite someone. He's a total disgrace to Dogdom. It would be a travesty for any family to put up with him. He'd give all dogs a bad reputation."

We now unmistakably realized we had to put him down. However, after three years of being with us, it was hard to kill him. Our sons knew of our decision to get rid of him, but didn't know of his possible death verdict. We were concerned also that our sons might fear if they misbehaved, they'd also be made to disappear. As an aside, this was before the Pooper Scooper law.

If this was in effect, we would've never put up with his shit. My wife and I argued over this dilemma endlessly.

We heard Bideawee (oldest pet adoption agency) would accept dogs, and guarantee they wouldn't put them to sleep. My wife eagerly called and lied, "We were leaving the area, and couldn't take our beloved dog." The administrator asked, "How old is he?" She answered, "Three." The secretary replied, "Unfortunately we don't take dogs over two." My wife responded, "He's so beautiful and has a pedigree with papers. Are there any exceptions?" The secretary answered, "Once a week our veterinarian evaluates new dogs with specific issues. If the dog qualifies, he may be accepted." My wife made the appointment knowing full well, Cavity couldn't possibly pass any behavioral test!

Since I had access to certain drugs, I found a possible solution to our predicament. I gave Cavity 25 mg of Valium just prior to his evaluation. - He was completely docile during the exam and behaved in a dream like trance. We guessed he must have been hallucinating about the other dogs. Astonishingly, he even licked the veterinarian. Cavity aced the test, we were ecstatic and high-tailed it out of there!

Three months later, my office secretary who knew of my ruse drove to the animal shelter, to find out if he'd been adopted. No he had not! She observed Cavity lying in his cell growling at his bowl of water. The attendant told her, "This dog was the only animal Bideawee had ever seen, that did this."

CERVICAL STRETCHING

Cervical stretching, not to be confused with cervix stretching, which I haven't experienced as yet – is the manual attempt to alleviate the compression of nerves in the upper part of the spine. In actuality, it's a pinched nerve in the neck, treated often with traction and wearing a cervical collar.

We all go through change as we age, so I thought I'd put into words some of the happenings going on in my life. I blissfully cut back on work and I'm now classified as semi – retired. Instead of going through life at 125mph, I've throttled down to 20-25mph. I now have more time for myself; having my neck manipulated in physical therapy three times a week. I thought I'd write this narrative, while my neck is being elongated.

I was diagnosed with "cervical radiculitis" which sounds a lot like cervical ridiculitis, which would be more fitting for me. I have always been a lover of the words and the absurd. My neck is being extended in a pilloried looking device that dates back to the 19th century. It's really a form of medieval torture. We've all seen these devices depicted in colonial times, as public punishment for some minor transgressions, such as cursing or drunkenness.

This particular device entails the use of ropes, weights and blocks mounted on a ceiling. The apparatus purportedly attempts to elongate your neck, so my cervical degenerative (I always like that word) discs won't impinge on my spinal nerves.

Fortunately, I am having rehab with a lovely woman, who never kvetches during our stretches. We alternate ten minutes on and ten minutes off. (We go neck and neck.) I'll finish up these double entendres by adding, "Both of us are tortuously involved, up to our necks in therapy."

I have minimal pain and intermittent paresthesia radiating down my left arm. (Fortunately, I'm right- handed.) Paresthesia is "the pins and needles feeling" you first experience when a dentist administers anesthesia. It conveys the onset of getting numb. I am a dentist and don't remember inadvertently giving myself, Novocain repeatedly, in my left hand.

Recently I received an inspirational memento from one of my cherished patients, after finishing her treatment. Jeanne and I had been philosophizing about life. (My job benefit allows me to do most of the talking, aided by laughing gas.) Her gift was a refrigerator magnet with a dowdy, frumpy photo of Eleanor Roosevelt. On it is one of her famous quotes that jumps out at you.

"DO ONE THING EVERY DAY THAT SCARES YOU."

Writing this diatribe scared me. It's the first time I've composed words for public viewing. Attempting anything creative takes courage, especially when the person cares about doing it right. Whatever age you are, it's still fun taking risks and in fact I did get an adrenalin rush playing with this. I hope you do something scary as Eleanor proposed – and think of me.

As an aside, I believe I grew a half inch since I started therapy and wrapping up this creative nonsense, "necking" hasn't been part of my treatment. – That would've been too far a stretch!

SPACE INVADERS

I hadn't lost more than a few days of work in over forty years as a dentist. Now I had an atrocious cold that wouldn't quit. I couldn't shake it and didn't understand why. My ten year old granddaughter Lauren was also showing cold symptoms. She wanted to talk to her "Pa" about what she might have to endure.

After a lengthy discussion of our plights, she thought she figured out why I got this cold.

Some background history is relevant. I am a mostly retired dentist; taking the winters off and working the rest of the year one day a week, in my son's dental practice. (formerly mine) Lauren's theory was my immune system is weaker because I work so little. Lauren might have gotten this epiphany from her father, my son the dentist discussing my situation, but I rather give her full credit for this revelation.

I believe a good immune system is a benefit from dentistry. Working very close to patients with the constant bombardment of pathogens in aerosol sprays, make dentists more resistant to sickness. Truly convinced my granddaughter was right, I tried to recreate an environment that would restore my immune system. I however, enjoy my very semi-retirement and don't want to increase the hours I work.

The natural solution to the problem is to mimic the dental environment with my daily personal contacts. If I get very, very close while conversing, the natural exchange of microbes should bolster my immune system. With friends I had the option of revealing why I was standing so close. However among new acquaintances, I didn't have that choice.

Trying this on close friends was interesting and fun for a while. Obviously, I did this tongue and cheek, without them knowing exactly what their playful buddy was up to. During conversations, I would start out at the normal distance of about four feet and gradually move closer. I'd aim for the normal dental position of about twelve inches. I would also try to initiate animated discussions, hoping they'd spray their words.

Every person has a boundary which other people may not cross. This is known as personal space. If an offender penetrates this space (i.e. talking) we feel uncomfortable and anxious. You could tell he ate garlic for lunch and feel the prickly hairs of his sweater. I've always wondered if these individuals are hard of hearing. As you move away, the offending party moves closer. You move away again, and he moves nearer. You get uneasy now and don't hear every word said. Inside you're screaming, "**GET THE HELL OUTTA HERE!"**

It has been shown different cultures have different "personal space" requirements. In highly populated continents (i.e. Asia or India) communication is conducted at much closer distances than in less populated countries like America. Perhaps, I should spend time in these foreign countries trying to improve my immunity? No, it would be too drastic a change for someone my age.

Applying this theory, I found old friends and new acquaintances had difficulties when I got preposterously close. I didn't like it myself. Trying to strengthen my immune system wasn't worth the consequences. I was losing friends and not making new ones. I was getting sick by the thought of former friends evading me! In semi retirement what should I do? Incongruously, some of my friends I'm really tired of, so I'm still evaluating.

Getting back to the topic, if this immunological hypothesis is shown to be valid, it could benefit mankind. Immune workshops could be developed by arranging people in small cubicles and engaging them in intimate communications. Every thirty minutes the participants rotate, exposing new pathogens. Dissimilar to dentistry where the dentist selects the subject, the patient undertaking treatment picks the topic. Theoretically each conversant should gain.

The next level of bolstering immunity would be to visit ailing people in hospitals where you'd interact with more virulent microbes. Besides ratcheting up your own defenses, you'd also be performing a *mitzvah* (good deed) by visiting sick people.

While putting my thoughts on paper, my cold got better. Since I really do enjoy my friends and country, I think the solution is to wear a NASA- like space suit, performing dentistry in semi-retirement. It'll allow me greater immune protection and I won't have to worry about invading anyone's space.

ACHILLES SPIEL

The Achilles heel of the Salmonson family just might be their Achilles heel. I just received a phone call from my forty year old son Scott. He ruptured his second Achilles tendon playing tennis and needs surgery again. He'll be on crutches for twelve weeks. What a horror! The first occurred seven years ago in the dead of winter. He had to deal with his commute to NYC, via the LIRR and subway. He couldn't drive a car (then it was his right tendon) and the snow, sleet and ice played havoc. Ironically, presently I'm undergoing therapy for my strained Achilles. When our kids were young, my wife also tore her Achilles. The cast from her foot to mid-thigh was on four months.

Achilles rupture is a quintessential major injury of aging athletes, whether they're elite professionals or weekend warriors. Many years of wear and tear has frayed the Achilles, leaving them vulnerable to that one sudden start when ……**snap**. The injury occurs in males 20:1 and most often happens between the ages of thirty to forty. The area doesn't heal well, because this largest of all tendons is poorly vascularized. It takes about six to twelve months to recover. The atrophied leg is noticeably weaker, smaller, and tighter for years. Depending on the activity, professional athletes have returned to their sport. Surprisingly, many were nearly as effective as before.

Legend has it; the mother of Achilles (mythological warrior) dipped him as an infant in the Styx River, while she held him by his heel. The river made him invulnerable wherever the water made contact. Hence, Achilles was indestructible, except for one spot - his heel. After numerous victories, he was killed by an arrow shot into his heel. As a result, the expression Achilles heel means a fatal vulnerability, or area of weakness i.e. kryptonite is Superman's Achilles heel.

Perusing the internet to find genetic connections to Achilles ruptures, I found a number of studies that confirmed this. The most valid paper was by a South African, named Michael Posthumus. (I'm not making this up.) This Posthumus study found a specific gene variant associated with Achilles heel tears. Individuals who carry this genotype have twice the risk. The study wasn't done posthumously!

After surgery Scott reflected, "You know you've had a bad week, when you have to borrow your Dad's walker." Incredibly, he seems to be dealing with this second setback relatively well. He stated, "It's given me an early perspective on the aging process." He can now better relate to handicapped people, as he graduates from wheel chair, to walker, crutches and eventually a cane. It has become an eye opener to what he might encounter getting older. He's also extremely grateful for his "handicapped parking sticker." Recently, he visited his kids at sleep away camp and greatly appreciated the handicap motel room with its conveniences for the disabled. In his next home he commented, "I'll definitely look for features that'll make a disability less incapacitating, like buying a ranch."

Following his second rupture, Scott now thinks he has his PhD in crutches 98% of the time. Conversely, 2% of the time he finds himself in some sort of near death experience. Additionally he's superb at hopping, which serves as an expediency whenever the situation is right. Of course, his favorite restaurant is "IHOP."

Some negative aspects of dealing with crutches include – being very dependent on others even for simple chores. Carrying things can be extremely difficult i.e. cup of coffee. Handling them is painfully insulting to your armpits and hands. It takes days to develop calluses, which follow after many painful hand blisters. You strain all kinds of muscles; you never knew you had. It also becomes tiresome listening to other people's stories about "crutches." Positives – turning on/off light switches and ringing doorbells.

Last night as Scott was driving home from work, there was a violent thunderstorm. It wasn't the downpour, making things slippery that made him apprehensive, but the bolts of lightning. He worried about being a human lightning rod because of his metal crutches. He said, "You never saw a handicapped person catapult so fast on crutches!! Finally home, totally soaked from the rainstorm and his own perspiration, Scott changed clothes. He was relieved to be safe and still alive. As he unwound from the harrowing day, he asked his wife for a glass of wine and some noshes; then another glass – then another.

Scott was now tipsy, but not approaching the state of stupor. (He knew he still lived in the state of N.Y.) He waxed philosophically about the possible derivations of Achilles heel clichés. Feeling no pain and ready to stand, he pondered the idiom "head over heels." Usually, it's associated with being in love. When first coined however, it referred to being literally upside down, perhaps from a violent fall. A similar meaning – topsy-turvy goes perfectly with his now being tipsy. "Always remember to put your right foot forward". This time he ruptured his left Achilles, but since he just had more than his share of alcohol, it wasn't a slam dunk which foot to use.

Scott now mellow became affectionate from the effects of the alcohol. However, the orthopedic cast, awkwardness and discomfort didn't contribute to love making. However, after the alcohol as I said he was feeling no pain. So ———

Later rethinking his day - the commute, thunderstorm, alcohol, and sex, he came up with a new proverb that surely should stand the test of time -

"While crutches support you after surgery, alcohol and crutches supports your return to the hospital."

DOUBLE DATING

My wife and I moved into an over fifty-five year old retirement community on Long Island. We knew from past experiences, we had to play the dating game with the new couples we'd meet. We enter these adventures feeling optimistic and open minded. However, we never get our hopes up too high that everyone will be compatible. After going out, my wife and I have a postdate locker room chat, reviewing these neighbors.

When a new foursome plays golf (two couples) there's less than a 25% chance the get-together will be successful. The group concludes affably only if all four get along and play well. If I like the guy and my wife doesn't, or my wife likes the woman and I don't, then a future for this foursome is a definite no-go. Therefore, the odds of the four making it are a long shot. After all, in the course of a lifetime, most couples are lucky if they have a handful or two of very good friends.

There's never enough emphasis on the importance of having friends in retirement. Social interactions are paramount in a well-rounded life after you've stopped working. Customarily, retirement considerations revolve mostly around finances. This of course is very important, but there are a host of other concerns that contribute to your happiness after you retire.

Once my wife or I, with some trepidation make the date, the stage is set for the meeting of the mates. In these uncharted waters, everyone is usually on their best behavior and tip toe through the formal greetings. We tend to think we're all experts on first impressions, but we've found it best to give the other person the benefit of doubt.

There are so many things that turn us off, it's a wonder we have any friends at all. Our tentacles are on high alert if the other couple tries excessively to impress us. Any areas of braggadocio send out radar signals for us to be on guard i.e. their brilliant kids, trips, life style and on and on. We've all been there! Equally annoying are those who love talking about themselves and have little interest in what you have to say. Now don't get me wrong, it's always fun talking about your own life and stories. We all know how we like virgin ears, so we can spew forth our own fabulous tales. But the proper balance of intercourse between the two couples is vital.

Another peeve of ours is the number of inappropriate cell phone calls the new couple might take. Besides being rude, it also reflects on your importance to them. I always wonder if they think the number of calls, serves as a testimonial to their popularity, position or status.

Does the pair have appropriate etiquette and respect for one other? Is there genuine warmth or is there underlying tension we're all familiar with? Also do they show propriety to you? All these factors are vital.

The first meal of the double date sets the table for further evaluations. Variables being scrutinized include the number of drinks, cost, and manners. Do you split the bill or tally each couple's separately? How much of a tip? Because it's a start of a potential relationship, each factor is looked at earnestly.

Is there a magical formula to assess the other couple? Absolutely not! "Chemistry" is the magical catch word which captures the intangibles for successful relationships. The more you have in common is always helpful, but not necessarily a deal breaker. Ironically, many friendships sometimes come out of nowhere. Our son became friendly with an Afro-American groundskeeper as they convalesced after both had major surgery. The two guys and spouses now enjoy each other's' company as a result of their life changing events. This intense situation and subsequent uninhibited emotional response, paved the way for friendship. You never know, and that's what makes every chance encounter interesting.

Should you settle? Each of us handles that question individually, although I guess most of the time you do. It depends on the number of so called friends you want around. Some people want a posse by their side and accept almost everyone. I suppose they assume having a lot of people around raises their social status. Others are content with fewer friends and having more meaningful relationships.

Fortunately, my mother – in- law who had been living with us moved into an independent living facility, just before we bought this new house. Otherwise, the article might've been called "Triple Dating."

I AM SO TIRED

I'm snoring?" I asked, after my wife elbowed me. "I can't take it anymore! Third time tonight I woke you" she bellowed, continuing "You got to see someone! I'm sleeping in the other bedroom."

Five years ago my wife injured her ears by repeatedly jamming ear plugs into them. She had tried every type, size and brand. Nothing worked well enough to adequately diminish my strident sounds. We even thought about going to JFK airport and purchasing ear mufflers, the ones attendants use taxiing planes to their gates. Surely, those pads though cumbersome should lessen the noise. She was not a happy camper. We were both losing sleep and constantly irritated. We were at a loss of what to do.

Often I'd wake myself, hearing my own snoring or gasping. At the time, I was sixty years old and getting up in the night frequently to urinate. Discussing this excessive urination with doctors and friends everyone assured, "It's normal for your age." Every time I'd rouse, especially in a sleep deprived state, I'd assume I had to urinate and did. I wasn't aware that waking (due to apnea) made me think (since I'm up) I must have to urinate. A

155

person with apnea rarely gets enough REMs (rapid eye movement phase) which is paramount for restful sleep.

I finally called a Sleep Clinic for more information. The center advised, "Telltale signs include loud snoring, male over sixty years old, hypertensive, overweight and large neck sizes; >17" males > 15" females." I realized I perfectly fit the description and registered for a nocturnal sleep study. The sleep doctor also recommended an exam by an ENT. (Ear, Nose and Throat, MD) The ENT can help if there are enlarged tonsils or adenoids. These obstructions could block breathing passages, contributing to sleep apnea.

At the clinic I befriended a sleep technician who told me two stories; a guy went to an ENT and was told without question he had an issue that could impact on his sleep. Returning to the sleep clinic he revealed, "The doctor told me I absolutely have a deviated rectum!" A woman was told by her ENT; her uvula (soft pendulous tissue hanging from the soft palate) was grossly enlarged and restricted her breathing. She revisited the sleep facility and divulged, "My vulva (female external genital organ) was huge and could be the problem!"

At the sleep clinic I was multi-wired and strapped to a number of monitors. (similar to a lie detector test) I'm not lying about this. Picture yourself trying to sleep in this setting; completely hooked up, tethered to a bed and in a totally unfamiliar environment. It took a half hour for the electrical leads to be placed. You're now imprisoned in bed. As I attempted to sleep, I realized I desperately needed to urinate. When I told the technicians, the grimaces on their faces were beyond description. I got out of bed and with an entourage of technicians, marched to the bathroom.

I stood at the urinal and next to me was a seven year old, doing the same. He also had sleep apnea because he wore the same armamentarium. We looked at each other and I could tell he didn't like what he saw. I said with a straight face, "Ya know, ya know, from what you look like I think we're related!" The kid dashed out, his member flying, screaming for his mother. I jolted out of the bathroom in my "Darth Vader Alien" outfit and sheepishly returned to my room.

Ironically, the next day the technician proclaimed, "You broke the university sleep center's record for falling asleep the fastest ever recorded." To this day I am very proud of that 24 sec. record. He also stated, "You stopped breathing thirty times during the night." Not too happy about that though.

The continuous positive airway pressure (CPAP) machine is the "gold standard" treating sleep apnea. However, there are a number of drawbacks. One always has a "bad hair day" as the device is tightly fastened to your head. You cannot have sex wearing this device, unless you're into "alien or Darth Vader sex." Really an acronym for CPAP should be "**Cannot Possibly Act Passionately.**" Traveling by plane with the CPAP machine can cause delays because some security agents have never seen this device. When I first transported the machine (after it was X-rayed) I was singled out and interrogated like a terrorist. Years later, after the agents became familiarized and the population of we "hose heads" climbed, one agent called the machine a "marriage saver."

A few surprising benefits do come with the machine i.e. having an instant Halloween costume. It also guaranteed to thwart any alien abduction. Did you know Osama Bin Laden was using his CPAP when the Navy SEALS entered his complex? The CPAP's whirring sounds helped drown the noise of his assassins. This medical device also gives me material for my stories.

Working in my dental office, Jack a friend I've treated for forty years became intrigued when I talked about my loud snoring and machine. "With the CPAP, my wife says I no longer make any noises at night." Jack chuckled, 'My wife complains I make sounds in my sleep too." Being generous, I offered Jack my appliance, hoping it'll solve his problem. Jack smiled, "No, no my wife says the noise comes from a different place... I fart all night." I told him, "That's still OK by me. Just put the CPAP machine in the right spot." We laughed and laughed and **could not stop**!

I asked the sleep physician, "Since loss of muscle tone exacerbates this problem, are there exercises to strengthen them?" She said excitedly, "I could practice singing, reciting or playing certain wind instruments. They're researching a reed musical instrument called the *Didgeridoo*. It's found in Australia and been used by the aborigines for 1500 years. It's about eight feet long and inexpensive. Researchers in Switzerland have gotten positive results teaching apnea patients to play it. It utilizes a circular breathing technique that strengthens these muscles. Patients have less severe episodes of sleep apnea."

Thinking entrepreneurially, I'm investigating the possibility of transporting a few Australian aborigines to teach *Didgeridoo* to our growing sleep deprived population. We would set up classes with heavy chairs (most people with sleep apnea are vastly overweight) and I even come up with a marketing slogan.

"If snoring is making your marriage go askew, the School of *Didgeridoo* might be the thing to do!"

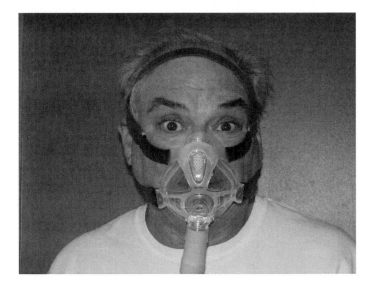

BUFFALO - 40TH DENTAL SCHOOL REUNION

With the eager excitement of a couple much younger, my wife Iris and I flew into Buffalo, where we met and fell in love. We fervently anticipated seeing old friends, haunts and reliving our history. It was 3PM and we were starving. As soon as we deplaned, the aroma of Duff's Buffalo Wings was redolent throughout the airport. We quickly picked up our bags and raced toward Duff's, the same restaurant President Obama had frequented. After overeating, our hands, clothes, mucous membranes, you name it, reeked from Buffalo wings. We brought this odor into our rented car, and sped to my 40th dental school reunion. Every five years, the dental school classes reconvene for a weekend of camaraderie and continuing education, which culminates with an impressive formal dinner dance.

In our foul fowl smelling car, we drove Niagara Falls Blvd. and headed straight to the campus book store. We always buy loads of memorabilia for ourselves and family to remind us of our undying love for this institution. From the ages of seventeen to past sixty-five, Buffalo has been a part of our lives. My wife and I both went to undergraduate and graduate schools there. (As an aside, we were fixed up on a blind date as sophomores, by my roommate's girlfriend Evie Lieberman. Evie was Hillary Clinton's secretary during the Monica Lewinsky scandal. She was first to warn Hillary about keeping Monica away from Bill.) We bought the usual T-shirts, coffee mugs, etc. but what really cracked us up – was buying a UB baseball cap. My wife had never seen a hat that was too large on me. These customized hats had numerical sizes; I tried on the largest. The cap immediately fell below my eyebrows and I couldn't see! Iris exploded with laughter and couldn't stop. This cracked me up and caused a chain reaction of laughter from the college kids watching these two ancient alumni. Remember, I had just stuffed myself with a humongous amount of Buffalo Wings. Hysterically laughing, I suddenly discharged a barrage of farts that further ratcheted up the laughter. These cyclical events caused another wave of laughter, farting that caused my wife to fly out of the book store, tears streaming down her cheeks totally mortified.

We toured the ever changing campus and returned to places we hung out. We revisited the city of Buffalo that like us had a much better past than future. We reminisced about our own early adolescent awakenings, which contrasted sharply with my present physical breakdowns. I was having knee replacement in a week, only four months after hip replacement. The rundown buildings, many boarded up, reminded me of my generation of friends and relatives. Years ago, everything seemed so alive, vibrant, and hopeful. Now Buffalo and I were sorely declining.

As the sun set we headed toward the Hyatt Hotel in downtown Buffalo. This upscale building headquartered both our reunion and the N.Y. Republican Governor candidate Carl Paladino. Election Day was two days away and Buffalo was the hot bed of his campaign. There was palpable excitement that kept the place hopping all night.

The next day, off we went to Niagara Falls, fully aware it

might be our last visit. This "wonder of the world" had undergone tremendous changes in our lives. We toured the majestic Falls, with its elevated vistas and world renowned floral decorations. Now up-to-the-minute casinos were interspersed between honky-tonk wax museums and T-shirt stores. Though it was my fortieth dental school anniversary, I realized we've been coming here almost fifty years. (freshmen undergraduates '62) Since nostalgia was running rampant, I recalled when the U.S. and Canadian governments cleaned up the Falls. The accumulation of rocks, trees, and debris decreased its visual beauty, not allowing it to run its full spectacular descent. The international committee used cranes, derricks, etc. to build a dam that diverted the Niagara River for this cleanup. I have an eerie photo of myself when the river was dammed. There's no water whatsoever, and I'm at the base of the Falls. From this spot, I vividly remember hearing the distant roar of the river. From the noise, I truly imagined the river getting closer and closer. I thought the dam thing broke!

The lecture series was capped (dental pun intended) off by my friend Harold Edelman, DDS. Never before had a good friend of mine addressed a large dental audience. Harold told Iris, "I've given this presentation fifteen years, but I'm nervous he might do something to embarrass me." As the lights dimmed with two hundred people in attendance, Harold asked me to stand and introduced me. He told the audience his fears of my being there. I timidly waved and sat knowing full well Harold had the power of the microphone. Though, I would never embarrass him, just the thought I made him anxious, made me smile. I took fifteen hours of continuing education over two grueling days. Sitting with my classmates reminded me of being a student in my early twenties.

Even though we had a small turnout, there were enough present to experience the reward of togetherness. It was also hard to believe two Hall of Fame dental instructors (Drs. Wiezkowski

161

and Garlapo) remembered me and asked how our son Eric (Buffalo dental grad '98)) was doing. It made us feel very special.

Micki Gianada, wife of our class president decided on the spur of the moment to have our class with spouses (about twenty) for dinner at their home. Bob Gianada told us unbeknownst to him, when he got up at 4AM for his constitutional, he heard pots and pans clamoring in the kitchen. He knew what Micki was doing. She cooked a complete dinner from soup to nuts and even baked a cake! It was one of the many highlights of the reunion.

The formal dinner dance required everyone to wear tuxedos and resulted in us looking the best we could possibly be. Our class of 1970 was seated most distant from the dance floor, positioned wisely closest to the bathroom. The dental honoree was the oldest dental school graduate, a mere ninety-five. As he spoke, we were shocked to discover he recently stopped working. We were also surprised his two grandsons who he worked with, were at tonight's event celebrating their 30th reunion. When asked, "Why did you retire?" He said in a barely audible voice, "I'm retiring because I'd like to spend more time with my grandsons." He paused and informed, "They're selling the practice and also retiring." The roar that emanated from the alumni; something I'll never forget!

On the wintry return flight, I mused how my love affair with Buffalo might've subliminally materialized. When television and I were barely past our infancies, I was obsessed with Howdy Doody, a puppet TV show. The program came to life from the creative mind of "Buffalo" Bob Smith, (from you know where) who also was a main character. Doody in my childhood vernacular meant; going to the bathroom. How could they get away with this absurd humor? The daily interactions between the puppets and adults jerked me around on a string. Clarabell, Flub-a-dub and Grandpa Doody, all hanging out in Doodyville! Cool Buffalo Bob blustering with Mr. Bluster. - That's where I want to be.

I'll run this by my psychiatrist.

THE SMILE MAKER

Here **lies the Smile Maker**, a Man who Loved Humor and Created Many Smiles." As I finish preparing my tombstone, I recognize it was my destiny to be involved with smiles.

My mother without hyperbole had the best laugh you ever heard. Beyond belief! Once she got going, she couldn't stop; her belly laugh took over the room. When she laughed, everyone got caught up in the euphoria. You'd laugh watching her laugh. She could've made a fortune in the old days before canned laughter, promoting a play, movie or TV show. She had an enormous toothy smile with large spaces between her front teeth. This automatically made her more comical, which aided her performances. I would do anything to get her to laugh. Early on I'd do slapstick, mime, absurdities, self- deprecation; you name it to get her started. From these early successes I realized I had a natural talent. Ironically, she bore this writer, who has the worst smile.

Growing up in Brooklyn, the passport to acceptance was humor. I assumed everyone thought comically. This wit developed by interacting with my many offbeat friends. Even today humor slants my outlook on life. Sometimes I wonder if this is normal.

The older kids in my neighborhood had different ideas of humor. Theirs included sarcasm, being caustic or acting just outright mean. If you had imperfections, (who doesn't) they'd zero in and relentlessly pick at them. Everything was fair game. They'd rank out your mother, father, target your sisters, etc. Many a tear resulted from this so called humor.

As fate would have it, Mom had an infatuation with our dentist. She followed him from his early Brooklyn location to Manhattan. We traipsed to Park Ave. by subway, which took an hour each way. I would double moan. First, the thought of going to the dentist and secondly, blowing the entire day, as we left early in the morning. Using her ingenuity, she did what most mothers would have done to shut me up. She bribed me saying, "I'll take you to our favorite lunch place."

"Don't eat for an hour" Dr. Siegel declared after every treatment. Therefore we had time to kill. My mother who at 5' 2" and about 180 lbs. had a special girdle store (including lingerie and underwear) in walking distance from our dentist. It was minute, the size of a kiosk, where we'd always go during that hour. At an early age, I hated this jam-packed store and often sat on the floor. As I matured (I was precocious) things were looking up from down there. When I was ten years old, I'd told my buddies, "This women's underwear store was getting better and better!" Now they wanted to change dentists so they could go!

My mother and I loved the Horn and Hardart Automat. It was mind-boggling, seeing all those mouthwatering foods in little windows, displayed in its walls. Equally fun was inserting nickels and dimes into slots, twisting the knobs and presto, it was yours for the taking. Although the hour had passed, often I was still partially numb. Intentionally, I'd dribble some food out of my mouth going for her laugh. Her uproars caused the other patrons to stop eating and crack up. I'd continue to eat and dribble as if I didn't know what was going on. She'd respond by having additional episodes of hysteria. The customers loved our show. Subconsciously, I actually enjoyed going to our dentist because of the two trips after our appointments.

I became enamored with Dr. Siegel's prestigious, highbrow mid-town office. I also fell in love with his gorgeous dental assistant, Nadia. I would rehearse my spittoon spitting at home, pretending I was numb, so I didn't look bad in front of this knockout lady. My friends cracked up watching me practice speaking to her and spitting, under the influence of imaginary "Novocain."

Our dentist's clientele were mostly professionals, dignitaries, and celebrities. One 8AM visit, I met (through Dr. Siegel's prearrangement) my hero Jackie Robinson. He treated his patients as friends and didn't place them on pedestals. I was always in awe of his stimulating conversations, banter and vocabulary. This inspiring man had a PhD in addition to his DDS. He practiced every phase of dentistry including orthodontics, root canals and implants, before specialization came into vogue. Additionally, he employed an in office technician, to fabricate cosmetic crowns. Dental manufacturers paid him to evaluate their products.

I was hooked and wanted to study dentistry. My dentist encouraged me and thought I had the appropriate personality and demeanor. Dr. Siegel, getting on in years, even suggested I take over his practice. I was more than thrilled. He became my mentor and visited me a few times in Buffalo, where I went to school.

In my sophomore year, I fell head over heels for Iris, my eventual wife. She has of course, an awesome, quick smile and a wonderful sense of humor. I pursued her tooth and nail. Subliminally, my love affair with smiles and teeth, directed me towards a woman with these gifts. To this day, her smile can be used as a weapon! And boy does she know how to use it!

After dental school and a two year stint in the Army, I returned to that Manhattan office to eventually take over Dr. Siegel's high-class practice. He was now in his mid-seventies and the timing seemed impeccable. He was the best dentist I had ever seen. I couldn't wait to be seventy, so I could be as good as he. (Be careful what you wish for; now I'm just about there.) Patients came from all over for his services. While working there, Jacqueline Kennedy and President Nixon called for appointments. I also believe he had more dentists as patients than any practitioner. He chortled, "Most dentists are the worst patients. They're the pits to work on." I learned a vast amount, but the practice wasn't transferable. Patients were coming to see him and only him. I was a rookie, in my late twenties and became his hygienist and assistant.

Eventually, I chose eastern Long Island for private practice and had a fulfilling career. I also taught at Stony Brook's dental school for ten years. While treating patients, I incorporated many of the techniques I learned from my mentor, especially in cosmetics.

My mother became my patient after Dr. Siegel died. She was having problems with her front tooth and saw me because she thought I wouldn't charge. As an aside, during my upbringing we had many tumultuous encounters. We battled on many fronts, as my mother was manic depressive before the term even evolved.

Mom's generation had a natural fear of dentistry because in their youth, they weren't given anesthesia, or when administered, it wasn't nearly as effective. She never forgot those painful encounters. Now working on her front tooth, with drill in hand I said, "Do you remember the time you.........to me?" She uncontrollably exploded with laughter!! She alarmingly remembered the more than a few times she mistreated me. Self-preservation, nature's foremost instinct arose, as she realized my implications. I was totally in charge and it was her front tooth no less. Past dental nightmares resurfaced. Mom's nervous laugh now joined her stupendous laugh. The synergy of the two resulted in an uproar that broke the sound barrier. She couldn't stop, couldn't stop! The entire staff, even people in the waiting room ran in to see what was happening.

Everyone enjoyed the show!

The legacy continues as our son became a dentist. Working with him has been the absolute high point of my career. He also loves doing cosmetics and orthodontics to perfect people's smiles. Ironically, he chose drsmiles@ optonline.net. as his email address. To think, it all started out with my mother's spectacular laugh!

SARA'S BAT MITZVAH

My granddaughter Sara recently had her Bat Mitzvah and celebratory party. The event was a milestone for her but also a benchmark for me. She's my first grandchild to participate in this ancient ritual, a child entering adulthood. Family and friends participated in this rite of passage following traditions that have been passed on for millennia. Sara is extremely bright, precocious, caring young lady on the precipice of taking her place in society.

Sara not only recited the difficult Torah reading, but flawlessly led the Saturday morning service, both in Hebrew and English. Her poise and elocution was picture perfect. While preparing for her Bat Mitzvah, she handled her public schooling extremely well by making the honor roll again. However, she did tell me, "At times, with everything going on, the thought of running away from home did cross my mind."

Blossoming into her teenage years, she was absolutely stunning, as the photos and videos will attest. I can visualize these same pictures being shown at her wedding someday.

Of course, it was by far the best Bat Mitzvah I ever attended.

This same sentiment echoed by her father Scott, was joyous to hear. (I recognize it's impossible to be objective, but I still wanted it stated.) The splendor of the venue, mouthwatering food, fantastic music all complemented by friends and family made an unparalleled affair. The band together with their dancers set the tone. The dance floor was packed with high steppers, revealing the youthful spirit of the crowd. Even the old folks reverted back to their former years, as they pounded away to the upbeat melodies. I though, unfortunately struggled because the following week I was scheduled for hip replacement. Ironically, the day after the merrymaking, a considerable number of people walked a lot like me!

Appropriately, I was given the honor of reciting the traditional blessing for wine, but struggled with its perception. At every Bar Mitzvah I ever attended, the male who chanted this ritual was past old. He often was escorted to the center of the room, where the *"alta cocker"* invariably shook and stuttered giving the *Borakhah*. (Hebrew blessing) As the old guy delivered, everyone sheepishly smiled. **Now this was me!**

My wife and I invited a dozen friends to the Bat Mitzvah. Two of the guys, amazingly were at my own Bar Mitzvah. Both married over forty years, we've been together with very few interruptions our entire lives. They were pleased we acknowledge them and we did truly enjoy sharing this moment.

Scott our older son, with microphone in hand gave some philosophy to his daughter. I was exceedingly proud, startled, and choked up as I heard these same values echoed to Sara, that I related to him many, many years ago.

Friday before the Bar Mitzvah, Sara shared the evening service with her good friend Beth. This petite almost teenager was having her Bat Mitzvah the following Thursday. Beth is physically challenged and looks much younger than her years. The natural warmth and chemistry exuded between the two honorees was magnificent to behold. Sara related to her as if she didn't have any disabilities. Then again, she always had this innate gift of easily interacting with the handicapped and I wouldn't be surprised if she went into this field.

My cardiologist had to be invited to this event. Dr. Levine happens to be a very good friend of Scott and daughter-in-law Lisa. This was one of the many reasons I chose to be his patient. He treats me like a member of his family. Before the extravaganza, Dr. Levine allowed his home to be used for a photo session for Sara and family.

Subconsciously, it was reassuring having my cardiologist there. I've always had the tendency "not to hold back, and push things to the max." My friend from kindergarten Gary also has this same propensity. After I introduced them Gary asked the doctor to watch over us. Their conversation ended with a spirited high five. Now we'd celebrate with no holds barred. We did ask Dr. Levine lightheartedly, if he could keep his partying down a few notches, so he could monitor us.

At the conclusion of the Bat Mitzvah, my wife took the dozen gorgeous long stemmed roses that centered our table. They were gigantic and beautifully assembled in a large heavy vase. As we were leaving, I couldn't find my valet ticket for our car. By chance, Dr. Levine was waiting for his car and also had taken the roses from his table. He saw me struggling and offered to hold my vase and flowers. As he balanced the two dozen roses, his face disappeared. (told you having your cardiologist around is helpful!) I then separated the flowers, found his eyes and moralized, "It's time to Stop and Smell the Roses."

The next day we returned to my son's house for brunch. Sara naturally exhausted, woke around 11 AM. Soon thereafter many of our relatives came. The kids flew upstairs to play in Sara's (their oldest cousin) bedroom. Sara was in the center having fun with all of them.

Witnessing this I couldn't stop thinking how this woman child Sara, was somewhere in the middle of this dichotomy. She was equally at ease playing with her young cousins, yet seamlessly broaching adulthood in her life's journey.

NG DDS

In forty years of dentistry I've done only a handful of house calls. Jeanne, a delightful patient and friend of thirty years phoned asking, "Could I do a favor?" Never wanting to say no, but with some uneasiness I inquired, "Sure, what' up?" "My grandmother is one hundred and her "centurial celebration" is in three hours. She never complains but told me she's very sore from her denture. I was hoping you could play Dr. Marcus Welby by coming over." Gathering my "doctor's bag" I drove the few miles to Jeanne's house where the old lady was staying. "Where is she?" I asked the sixty year old granddaughter. "Upstairs, getting dolled up!" as she pointed. Amazed the old granny was using the bedroom one flight up, I climbed the steps as my knees and stairs creaked. I was flabbergasted when I saw the honoree. Her six foot robust frame rose and gave me the firmest of handshakes, as she got off the computer!

For the past three years I've been semi-retired, working one day in our family practice. The office is located near Leisure Village, a large over fifty-five year old Long Island community opened in 1970. Three years later I began my practice. Therefore doing the math, I've seen some of these patients forty years. Our office may have the most over ninety year olds on Long Island. They give new meaning to "old patients and old friends." Although this writer is approaching seventy, I often feel like a kindergartener, as I attend more hundred year old festivities than anyone you know.

Dentistry lends itself to "Being close up and personal." It might be the most intimate of all the health professions. Due to the patient proximity and repeat nature I've teased, "Over all these years, I've been closer to you than just about any person in your life." Many of them can't hear, don't understand, but I still like the thought.

I have emerged in our practice as the nonagenariandontist. No such word yet but it'll mean "dentist who works specifically on patients over ninety." This invented word is way too cumbersome, so I shortened it, from nonagenariandontist to a "NG, DDS." However, I don't limit my practice solely to this age group. I also see patients in their seventies who are called the "pediatric" segment of my NG dentistry practice.

The actual dentistry performed on these senior, senior citizens is usually easier than general dentistry. They're not as demanding and more concerned with function. With their loss of visual acuity, and knowing their own life expectancies, cosmetic dentistry is less important. Though unbelievably I had one ninety year old woman state and I think seriously, "The only time I go to a doctor is for plastic surgery."

Pragmatically, I don't worry about my restorations lasting more than ten years or so. I banter "I guarantee my work for a lifetime." Adding, "Whose lifetime, yours or mine?" Fortunately, both this dentist and these patients usually don't remember what was said. Incidentally, the nonagenarian discount is slightly higher than those to regular senior citizens. They're greatly appreciative as often there's financial concerns. I encourage this group (over 90 yr. olds communicating could be a marvelous TV skit) to tell their fellow nonagenarians about this special bonus.

It's a win-win situation for both this population and older dentists. Nonagenarians will double by 2030 and quadruple by 2050. These very old patients are usually more comfortably treated by someone closer to their age. Semi-retired dentists definitely have more time to treat them. This helps because we both move quite slowly, and don't hear well. My son runs our busy practice and can't give the very elderly as much time to schmooze. Fortunately, most elderly dentists don't have to generate as much income in semi-retirement. Older NG dentists can also relate better to a nonagenarian's medical issues. Geriatric patients have different problems i.e. rampant decay and root caries. This can occur due to dementia, poor manual dexterity or non-existent hygiene. This NG DDS has become their caretaker maintaining their dentitions and avoiding infections. It's a way of giving back to greatly appreciated patients who've been with me forever.

As a result of the rising geriatric population there's a shortage of dentists who treat them. Geriatric dentistry is rarely selected by young practitioners. Young dentists often have crippling graduation debts and may focus on production. In addition, older dentists are more experienced in removable dentistry. Fabricating false teeth is a lost art as fewer patients are edentulous. The amount of time studying removable dentistry by younger dentists is significantly less than the old timers.

Being semi-retired is similar to experiencing my second childhood. I wonder if nonagenarians are back there too. (Obviously, some are closer to infancy.) I thank these special patients and speculate about their secrets to longevity. Working part-time with people who've been with me forever is a treat I never expected.

I rate myself a good NG DDS, who sometimes has to make godlike decisions in choosing their proper treatment. It has been an honor and privilege to help these nonagenarian friends.

WEDDING MUSES

I **love wedding** parties and I know you do too. How can you not love the jubilation, food and merrymaking? These affairs are fueled by friends, relatives, music and the free flowing alcohol. It's hard to imagine a wedding not being enjoyable.

My earliest wedding recollections go back to when I was about ten years old. At these affairs, my older male relatives would joke and tell

stories that were over my head. My "big" cousins swirled their Cokes (so I thought) as they bantered. They'd smirk, laugh – I just stood there. I'd have that glazed look; not having a clue what they were talking about. Looking back, it was a rite of passage. Being the youngest of many cousins I was enlightened by my cousin

Herbert, brought to this earth one year before me, informing "Alcohol was in their drinks!"

Always precocious and inquisitive, I had to discover what was so special about those drinks that made their eyes twinkle and made my cousins so cheerful. Consequently, I swiped one from my absolutely blitzed Uncle Murray whose drink resembled my cousins; then another and another. As a result, Murray kept ordering more and more alcohol. His wife Anna, who had a few herself, was unaware I'd been taking his, hauled off and smacked him yelling, "I can't believe how many drinks you had! You can't drive us home." I then proceeded to tell my cousins the "Uncle Murray-Auntie Anna" story. My cousins ran over to watch the scuffle. I was now officially initiated into my cousins' circle. As a result, Rum & Coke became the drink of choice for this ten year old.

Since dancing came easy and everyone was on the dance floor, I took a giant swig of my Rum and Coke and ventured out to have some fun. Not knowing why, drinking Rum & Cokes coincided with my dancing uninhibitedly. At every affair there always seemed to be a crowd watching me Rock 'N' Roll. Not surprisingly a few years later, when my hormones kicked in, I tried slow dancing. Obsessing about sex every minute, I had no control of my equipment. Needless to say, even with loose pants, I had conspicuous problems slow dancing.

I was twelve at the time of my favorite cousin Martin's (He took me to my first Brooklyn Dodger game.) marriage. I now had turned pro taking Rum & Cokes. Logic told me if I'm this good, why not feel better and have more. After all, the rules of life never pertained to me. I was having a ball, goofing with my cousins and dancing as if I was the only one out there. As a result, my relatives were having more entertainment with me than usual. I got loosey- goosey, giddy, and then outrageous.

My drinking beckoned a call to the bathroom. It was strange

for the first time ever, having difficulty walking, even talking for that matter. It was even stranger meeting my father on the way to the men's room. I didn't like the look in his eyes when I attempted to talk. Then the room spun and nausea kicked in. I got sick, sick big time and then violently ill. Vomiting repeatedly, I had to stay in the bathroom the rest of the wedding. Throwing up from alcohol was also a rite of passage, even though I wasn't right at all! – My father never left.

The next day, I learned what a hangover was and was surprised when my father came to talk. Dad was a huge man, a physical laborer, stronger than any father out there. After we spoke, my eyes averting his, I apologized and said, "It won't happen again." He said, "Here's something to always remind you." I was completely surprised, stunned and then staggered when he hauled off and whacked me. Never before or ever since, had he ever hit me. It hurt all right, but when you get backhanded by your father, the pain lasts far longer than the bruises. I can still feel it.

THANK YOU LETTER

I want to express my gratitude to Jean, a Valencia Falls writing club colleague for choosing the assignment "write a thank you letter." I know in the most important decision of my life, selecting a wife, I've partnered exquisitely. I thank my right mate Iris even though she's lefty. Too often time passes and thank yous are never mentioned on paper.

I've often wondered about fate and the role it played in our getting together. If it hadn't been for something stupid I did in high school, most likely we never would've met. And if it weren't for Iris' encouragement to participate in this writing club, she probably wouldn't be the recipient of this tribute. Inherently, we're all aware time outs should be called periodically to document these "thank yous. Time to do this though, often sadly fades. As we get older we tend to put on a few pounds and get schmaltzy in our thoughts. However, I hope this thank you note isn't reminiscent of an unoriginal Hallmark card.

"The secret of life is enjoying the passage of time." - James Taylor. Life is captivating because each chapter is unique and no one has traveled these roads before. It's filled with pleasures, sorrows, angst and ecstasies. I've been very fortunate that you've been my sounding board and helped in decision makings since we're nineteen.

As we age time accelerates to an alarming pace. Retirement can allow you to slow it down and reflect on life. It's a major benefit of withdrawing from the work force. It has allowed me to give you more time and present this acknowledgment.

The years have been a friend to you. Your beautiful smile is full of warmth and lights up every room you enter. Your art ability colors and sculpts my view of the world. You've been gifted with so many attributes that in my mind you've won the genetic lottery. Discreetly and humbly, I've always tried to restrain bragging about your scores of talents. Possibly your best gift, is giving whole heartedly to the people around you and making them feel as if they're the only one present.

I remember the first day I saw you as if it was yesterday. With soft cascading hair hanging down your shoulders and a figure commanding my eyes, my heart reacted like a run-away train. You awakened me and made me feel most alive. Now it's almost fifty years that we've traversed the tangled trails of time. My heart will keep on chugging for you until the pump gets too frail or hospice knocks. There'll be other days and other things to say but while there's still some ticking; let me put it in writing.

– An abundance of thanks

What is love? Passion, admiration, and respect. If you have two, you have enough. If you have all three you don't have to die to go to heaven. – Anonymous

A NATIONAL PARK PERK - ARCHES

My wife Iris and I are passionate about exploring our National Parks. Twenty years ago we toured Arches in Moab, Utah with its spectacular red sandstone rock formations manifested in its mesas, buttes and of course arches.

We arrived at the park early and immediately noticed loads of photographic equipment. We assumed it was a photo shoot for a fashion magazine (Vogue or Elle) in this idyllic setting. The Park Ranger disclosed they were filming "City Slickers II" and the crew was nearby. Knowing Billy Crystal was starring, and with camera in hand, we took off to find the motion picture company. We're huge fans of this Hall of Fame comedian.

Without difficulty we found the film company, which happened to be on break. Surprisingly, there were no tourists around. Close by the comic Jon Lovitz was using his video camera, to record this picturesque park. Billy Crystal was by his side, doing the audio for Lovitz' personal video. As I sheepishly took their photos, we cracked up listening to their banter and fun. It was surreal watching these two great stars playing like kids. Though I felt like a bashful intruder, I couldn't stop clicking their pictures. Billy

Crystal watching us react, got into it more and more. We were shocked; they were performing for an audience of two. Billy said to Lovitz, "Why don't you take a video of that guy (this writer) and wave." Picture the scene in your mind's eye. My photo came out much better than that!

Billy Crystal came over and asked shyly, "What are you guys doing here?" I replied, "We're from Long Island and on vacation." I immediately added, "By the way, my wife went to high school near Long Beach." (Crystal's home town) Billy's eyes lit up as he inquired, "Who do you know from Long Beach?" Iris responded, "I'm a bit older, so you may not know the people I hung out with." Billy quickly retorted, "No, no I have two older brothers who I tagged along with and both still live in Long Beach." Iris gave a litany of names. He responded, "Some of the names do sound familiar."

I burst into the conversation exploding, "My roommate in college was Sticks." (Billy Crystal was a very good athlete who played basketball and baseball.) Crystal always looked up to Sticks both literally and figuratively. Billy Gordon (Sticks) at the time was 6' 4" about 170 lbs. captained their basketball team. Though Sticks was three years older, they'd often play ball at their local school yard. After college Sticks returned to Long Beach and took over his father's pharmacy. Instantaneously, Billy Crystal's face lit up and grinned from ear to ear. I followed, "I played basketball with Sticks at Buffalo, all the time.

"Can't You Tell?"

Picture what Billy Crystal was looking at! I was about fifty years old and seventy pounds overweight from my ball bouncing days. My hair pattern can best be described as a "bald eagle" and I had a sizeable paunch. Billy Crystal looked at me and cracked up. He laughed and laughed. "I absolutely love that line!" he said. Needless to say, I was so proud making this marvelous comedian LOL.

Now Billy wants to know all the people I knew from Long Beach and how they're doing. We had about a dozen names in common and Crystal wanted to know each and every story. We must have spoken for twenty minutes. He became very relaxed and confided, "We've been here six weeks, winding down, but getting bored." I almost asked, "Where are you staying and maybe we'll stop by?" My wife would have killed me if I did. I did ask though, "Can I take a picture of you and my wife? "Sure" he replied.

We left exhilarated beyond words and high from the amazing conversation with this much admired superstar. We were also impressed with how down to earth he was.

Hours later still reveling, I told Iris I forgot to tell Crystal about other people I remembered from Long Beach. Additionally, I should have told Jon Lovitz, one of our best friends has his same name! I pleaded, "Let's go back and find them." Iris of course, thought I was more nuts than usual and worried Billy Crystal would think we're stalking him. Using my relentless persuasion, I convinced her to drive back. Unfortunately, the movie crew was not at their former location. We searched and searched and just before we gave up, we found them!

Serendipitously, the actors were on break again. This time Jon Lovitz was alone, sixty yards away, again taking home videos. I called out, "Do you need someone to do the audio since Billy's not here?" 'Sure,' he smiled. Not believing what was happening, I ambled up to Lovitz and rambled into his camera about the breathtaking beauty of the arches, canyons, and "my newly found friends." I must say, I did a decent job, not quite as good as Billy Crystal, but Lovitz was smiling! As we walked back to the film site, I confessed, "One of the reasons we came back, was to tell you, my best friend has your same name." Lovitz looked at me astonished, and with his nasal inflection delivered his signature line, "Oh yea, oh yea, does he think he's me?" I cracked up, as I never expected him to play with me! He then asked, "How does he spell his name?" I spelled it LOVETT, not realizing the names were close but no cigar. The comedian never said a word! Later after I embarrassingly realized my error, I suspected Lovitz thought, "That idiot doesn't even know my name." As we returned to the set I asked, "What's the story with Jack Palance? He seems to be losing it." Palance won the best supporting actor in the original City Slickers at the Academy Awards. Before accepting his Oscar, the 73 year old did one handed push-ups, and acted erratically on TV. Lovitz tactfully replied, "Jack Palance is a great actor who has served the industry for over fifty years." I was so impressed Lovitz protected his fellow performer with class and sensitivity!

A tall good looking guy who I didn't recognize strolled toward us as we returned to the set. I remembered seeing him when I talked to Crystal and Lovitz. I presumed after spending so much time with the two comedians he was dying to know who I was. I just brushed him off! Later I learned it was the well-known actor Daniel Stern, who appeared with Joe Pesci in the hit movie "Home Alone." He was also the melodious voice on the long running TV show "Wonder Years."

We returned to the set and saw Billy Crystal again. After waving, I stopped and asked, "By any chance, do you need any extras in the film?" Surprisingly Billy pointed and said, "Yea, climb that plateau and act like a tourist." I dashed over and two scrawny crew members tried to lift this 210lb. load. I was more than concerned this heavy-weight would pull both of them down. After a treacherous effort, I made it to the top, but unfortunately the scene was cut.

The pictures at Arches National Park came out better than anticipated. I dragged the photos everywhere and retold the story hundreds of times. Just by chance my Aunt Mim and Uncle Hank had their 50th anniversary party. I brought the 11" X 14" pictures of course and showed them to my cousins. They were flabbergasted! I also showed the full page photo of Iris and Billy Crystal to my Uncle Hank. Iris and I had been married over thirty years at the time and she'd been to every family party, wedding, etc. Uncle Hank had spoken to her at each and every one of these occasions. Hank was now eighty and maybe starting to lose it. After showing him the picture of the two, I asked, "Who is this?" He looked carefully and thought and thought. He then said, "She looks very, very familiar!" I doubled over laughing and proceeded to tell everyone his reply. We all rolled!

Iris' birthday was coming up. Unbeknownst to her, I called my college friend Sticks and told him the stories of Arches, Crystal and my Uncle Hank. I asked Sticks if there was any possibility of getting Billy Crystal to sign this phenomenal picture. Sticks contacted Crystal's brother, who as I said lived in Long Beach. The brother hesitantly gave the address.

I sent the large picture with a return envelope. Inside, I wrote the story of the 50th anniversary and my Uncle's response. Billy returned the photo signed "To Iris, Happy Birthday! With my best wishes, Billy Crystal"

On the picture he placed a sticky "post-it" saying,

"Maybe I'll use that story!"

AN EERIE, EARY 911

Lady, lady!" **he** hollered —"Don't let'em piss on my lawn!" This was the way Phyllis' day began, restraining her two grand-dogs (her daughter's large Labradors) as they pulled and pranced about, while wheeling her two year old granddaughter in her baby carriage. That shout emanated from an obese curmudgeon who lived a few houses away. She heard the troublemaker was over ninety years old and surprisingly, still married. He had a face as the saying goes, makes you realize God has a sense of humor. Everyone on the block heard his incessant bellowing and screaming. "If those dogs make my lawn brown, you'll pay for a new one," he screeched. Mortified, Phyllis juggled her brood and hightailed it out of there, hoping they wouldn't go on his grass. Not a good way to start your day.

Phyllis is a youthful grandmother who unhappily just started to wear hearing aids. Sadly, as most with this particular problem will attest, she's constantly trying new hearing aids, batteries, etc. in an effort to hear better.

Three days after this incident, Phyllis had a particularly harrowing day. At 8 AM she dashed to her hearing specialist, to have the new aids tweaked again. At 9:30 she was needed by the same daughter to baby sit and walk her dogs. As she locked the door holding her paraphernalia i.e. keys, leashes, plastic bags, pooper scooper, cell phone, she just about heard someone pleading, "Help, Help me! Help!"

She ran down the driveway and called.....".Where are you... where are you?" Frantic, Phyllis couldn't locate where the faint cry was coming from. With baby carriage and dogs in tow she rushed down the street. Three houses away, she saw that ninety year old neighbor on the floor. It was the same old guy who yelled at her when she previously walked the dogs. He laid spread eagle in his doorway, half way in and out, with little clothes on. He implored, "I can't stand up, go in the house and call 911." Even though the grouch had screamed at her, she knew she had to help.

Phyllis said, "I have a cell phone and besides I'm not going into your house with the dogs." In that instant Phyllis realized the dogs hadn't done their duty since yesterday and were more than due. Turd tension was in the air for both Phyllis and the dogs. She hoped this wouldn't influence her decision makings in this harrowing dilemma. "Please, you must help me," he sobbed.

Now picture the scenario, the two dogs barking and yanking, baby bawling, and the old guy on the floor begging. Juggling everything, she dialed 911. With the phone next to her ear, loud static emanated from the batteries in the hearing aids and her cell phone. She then positioned the phone at a forty-five degree angle, attempting to hear the operator. Phyllis spewed out in frenzy, "My neighbor is on the floor and can't get up." Without pausing, she shouted her name, address and other important information. Because of the interference she couldn't hear, but surmised what the operator needed to know to come ASAP. Faintly she heard the operator say, "Ma'am, ma'am stop talking.....stop talking, you're going too fast." Phyllis responded, "I'm deaf and can't hear you!" The operator repeated louder, "Ma'am, ma'am STOP

TALKING." Phyllis blurted out, "Okay, okay, wait a minute; I'll remove my hearing aids." With her hands full, as she took them out, the batteries from the hearing aids flew out. Now she pressed the phone as tightly as humanly possible to her ears and said, "Okay, I'll try to listen, but talk LOUD!"

The operator asked, "How old is the man?" Phyllis looked hard but only focused on his face. Deaf people try very hard to read lips, as she asked him. "I'm ninety- one," he replied, which she repeated to 911. Then the operator asked, "Is he in the house or out?" Now Phyllis had to look at ALL of him. As she looked at his exact location she answered, "Well he's half in and —- Oh my God, Oh my God he's naked!"

Gaining composure, Phyllis looked at the man and saw he was completely exposed. She asked him, "Do you want me to get a blanket?" He said, "Why, I don't need one I'm not cold." She responded, "But you don't have any clothes on." Phyllis wondered if the guy had Alzheimer's or perhaps he's a semi-retired flasher. Being considerate, she grabbed the baby's blanket and covered his penis, surprised how little it was.

Phyllis hung up the phone and waited for the ambulance. Holding the screaming baby, she walked the dogs staying close to the guy. Her mind wandered …."I've had a very sheltered life. I met my husband at nineteen and he's the only male I've ever seen. Movies and real life aren't the same." The old fat guy's penis was astonishingly small. In old age, Phyllis knew our bodies revert back to the days before puberty, but this was ridiculous. While in this surreal state, she remembered a girlfriend telling her, "For every thirty pounds of being overweight, there's apparent one inch penis shrinkage." Confirming these facts she recognized, "The tools of love really do wear down."

Now the dogs were really desperate to defecate. They did their thing, but unfortunately they went ridiculously close to where the guy's head was grounded. The Labs and she were greatly relieved, but not the old fart. Phyllis left the scene, still holding the crying baby to get plastic bags to clean up. When she returned he roared incomprehensibly, "Didn't I warn you - don't let your dogs shit on my lawn?" Phyllis, totally pissed let loose, "When you're up to your nose in shit, keep your mouth shut!"

Phyllis calmed the baby and placed her in the carriage. (Fortunately it was a hot day and the grandchild didn't need her blanket.) She then re-inserted the batteries and placed her hearing aids back.

The old guy then proceeded to bawl like her grandchild, "My wife had a stroke yesterday. We've been married sixty years; I can't do anything without her! I fell as I was dressing to visit her. I dragged myself out the door." (Phyllis never asked why he didn't crawl to the phone in his house.)

When the 911 team arrived, he told the paramedics, "Get me off the floor so I can drive to the hospital to see my wife. I got to see her, she had a stroke." The EMT asked, "Where is she?" Stammering, he faltered, "I —I —I can't remember." They loaded him in the ambulance and the crowd started to disperse. Phyllis noticed she was the only one who didn't put her hands to her ears when the ambulance (sirens and lights in full force) departed. Phyllis watched the vehicle disappear, took a deep breath, relieved that crisis was over. She went back to the hyperactive dogs and tried to comfort her grandchild, who was howling again.

Phyllis finished telling me the story - her shoulders slumped. The writer asked, "What happened to the old man and wife?" Phyllis spoke softly and said, "I'm very ashamed to say I never found out. I should've phoned the hospital or gone to his house but didn't. I feel really bad."

"Ashamed?" the writer questioned. "You're a great Samaritan; you did everything textbook in a preposterous situation. You're now fixated on the one negative that transpired." Isn't it strange even after a heroic job we focus on the things that went wrong?

We often beat ourselves up dwelling, lamenting, and rehashing the miniscule things that didn't go right. Why is this built into our psyches? Does this self-flagellation serve any useful purpose?

The writer told Phyllis the only way to resolve the quandary was to contact this nasty guy. Weeks later, Phyllis knocked on his door. He was completely ecstatic and shouted, "You've saved my life!" You wouldn't believe what happened next!

To be continued......